C000215107

The British Bloke

DECODED

The British Bloke

DECODED

**From Banter to Man Flu.
Everything finally explained.**

GEOFF NORCOTT

monoray

First published in Great Britain in 2023 by Monoray, an imprint of
Octopus Publishing Group Ltd
Carmelite House
50 Victoria Embankment
London EC4Y 0DZ
www.octopusbooks.co.uk

An Hachette UK Company
www.hachette.co.uk

Text copyright © Geoff Norcott 2023
Illustrations copyright © David Eldridge 2023

All rights reserved. No part of this work may be reproduced or utilised in any form or by any means, electronic or mechanical, including photocopying, recording or by any information storage and retrieval system, without the prior written permission of the publisher.

Geoff Norcott has asserted his right under the Copyright, Designs and Patents Act 1988 to be identified as the author of this work.

ISBN 978-1-80096-129-6

A CIP catalogue record for this book is available from the British Library.

Printed and bound in Great Britain

1 3 5 7 9 10 8 6 4 2

Typeset in 11/15pt Sabon LT Pro by Jouve (UK), Milton Keynes

This FSC® label means that materials used
for the product have been responsibly sourced

MIX
Paper | Supporting
responsible forestry
FSC® C104740

This monoray book was crafted and published by Jake Lingwood, Pauline Bache, Liz Marvin, Mel Four, David Eldridge and Peter Hunt

*I'd like to thank my lovely
wife and brilliant son for
not only accepting the bloke
I am but making me want
to become a better one.*

AUTHOR'S NOTE

In this book, you'll encounter language which, in certain circles, might be deemed a bit old-fashioned. For example, I sometimes refer to my wife as 'the Mrs'. She's fine with that, as are most women I know, but some might consider those words a relic from the seventies – possibly like the average bloke himself. In a way, that's the point of this book. I want to examine aspects of the British Bloke which have evolved dramatically in recent years, while also acknowledging that, in other senses, we might not have changed so much at all.

In thinking about 'the bloke', I've often found myself pulling apart the dynamic between straight men and straight women, which I know could be seen by modern standards as not especially inclusive. However, in a time when writers are encouraged to 'stay in their lane', the 'heteronormative' lane is the only lane I've ever known. I'm not trying to exclude any tribe, just trying to make sense of my own.

So, whoever you are, I hope this book resonates with you as we find out more about that singular enigma – the British Bloke.

'You tried your best and you failed miserably. The lesson is never try.'
Homer J Simpson

PROLOGUE

Last autumn, I was picking up my six-year-old son from one of his many after-school clubs. We were talking about a playground incident which had happened earlier in the day. He'd been playing a tag-based pursuit game with his mates, but a couple of the lads had such physical pace it was virtually impossible for the other boys to win. So my son, with his top-notch brain, had cleverly rejigged the rules in order to make it a bit fairer.

The act of play colliding with cold, hard bureaucracy isn't unusual for boys of this age. For a six-year-old lad, one of the great joys of playtime isn't just the game itself but a level of needless officialdom which would make local government blush.

The faster boys eventually worked out my son's game and started to tease a little, which had him rattled.

I smiled, confident my paternal wisdom could reassure him about what had occurred. 'Son, it's fine,' I reassured him, 'All that's happened is you've had your first bit of banter.'

Before I even checked his reaction in the rear-view mirror, I could hear the finely tuned cogs of his mind whirring.

'What's banter?' he asked, his brow furrowing in a way I hadn't seen before.

I warmed to my explanation, happy to help him take his first steps into a bigger world.

'Son, banter is when your mates take the mickey out of you, it's part of friendship.'

More silence. His cogs whirred louder still and I began to flounder.

'Erm, in a group of mates, one way the other lads will assess your worth as a male is by how much banter you can take. If you can take a bit of stick they'll . . . sort of . . . know you're a good guy, because they can depend on you to stand up . . . under pressure.'

He started glancing out of the window, his subtle way of letting me know I was losing him. I started to reach further.

'I think banter evolved from when men would go out hunting. They'd be a long way from the camp and would need to know the other fellas were strong, so would test them out. Maybe in the past we'd do it physically but now we do it with words . . . it's all about not showing weakness to the tribe, you see.'

There was a long pause as he digested everything I'd said and came to a conclusion.

'I don't like banter,' he said, 'it's not fun.'

He promptly returned to looking out of the window at the dark sky and amber lights whizzing by.

Presented with the first challenge of communicating one of the central pillars of blokeyness to my son, I'd fumbled it. I'd taken what should have been a simple idea and introduced needless levels of complexity and concern. Instead of allowing his playtime event to simply be an awkward moment at school, I'd used so many hunting metaphors he must've been wondering if I'd decided it was time for his first kill.

I take being a father to a son seriously, particularly at such a confusing time for boys. Being male is one of my few areas of genuine expertise. As a bloke, I've now clocked up forty-six years of unbroken service. I dress very blokily, typically in jeans and a polo shirt. My image is so middle-of-the-road that when I do my stand-up comedy shows, I look like a ticket tout for my own gig, the kind of guy who might not know much about jokes but would definitely know where to order a skip.

Furthermore, I recently discovered I literally *am* the average bloke, certainly on a statistical basis.

I'm five foot nine (OK, five foot eight and a half) (OK, a quarter). My feet are a decidedly average size nine. I weigh thirteen and a quarter stone – and yes, my other proportions are decidedly average too. In recent elections, I've voted pretty much in line with the majority of the country. My favourite food is curry. My favourite sport is football. My favourite sitcom is – you've guessed it – *Only Fools and Horses*. My favourite documentary? *The Story of Only Fools and Horses*.

I am a route-one bloke who finds comfort and distraction in simple things.

Tesco released the most popular combination of their meal deal. Guess who'd bought a ham and cheese sandwich, cheese and onion crisps, and a Diet Coke for the last fifteen years? (And, incidentally, never got bored, though I sometimes swap out the crisps for Mini Cheddars if I'm feeling reckless.)

Even on a class basis, I'm one of swathes of people who was brought up in a working-class environment but now enjoys the trappings of a more middle-class existence. In another time, I'd have been called 'Mondeo Man' (if he didn't sound like the world's shittest superhero).

All my life I've been dimly aware that I've been cursed – or blessed – with a radical form of mediocrity, so if there's one thing I know a lot about it's being a standard bloke, and a British one in particular.

It's been a testing time for the male brand of late. In the last few years, the term 'Men' (as opposed to 'blokes') has become something of a pejorative one implying privilege and power. There was a long overdue reckoning for certain kinds of toxic men who needed taking down a peg or two: men who leched, men who waged wars . . . men who were Matt Hancock. However, as I started to think about this book, I realised there was a world of difference between those guys – who never spoke for the vast majority – and the standard British Bloke. But, as feminism found renewed energy in the second half of the 2010s, all the valid discourse also created a slipstream which other things fell into.

It's true that the list of people who've crashed economies and started wars mostly contains people who could pee standing up. But meanwhile, the other 99.9 per cent of their sex were, at worst, crashing Ford Fiestas or starting DIY projects they never finished.

So forgive me if I exclude blokes from some of the wider excesses of the male species. The vast majority of us have never harboured any desire to hold political power and the nuclear codes – and if we were given them we'd probably palm them straight off to our wives. It's safer that way. She's always done a pretty good job with the passports.

I can't speak for a whole sex, but when it comes to the sub-genre of 'blokes' I've given it a lot of thought and the good news is we might not be so bad after all. I'm beginning to think that, beneath the farting, grunting and general inattentiveness, there's a lot more to us than meets the eye. The underlying complexities of explaining banter to my son illustrate that point. Once I'd realised that something as seemingly simple as ribbing your mates was underpinned by such complicated motives, I went down a rabbit hole thinking about other blokeish things which also have hidden depths (just like, I strongly believe, blokes themselves).

So the plan with *The British Bloke Decoded* is to investigate all those unexpectedly complex intricacies of the male experience and get to the bottom of them. To unpack and decode British blokes, looking at those apparently still waters and wondering what manner of mad shit is scuttling around beneath.

Over fifty or so chapters, I've taken on subjects from man flu and lager to crying and losing friends in an effort to understand what really makes the British bloke tick. There are important questions here that need answering. What is the enduring appeal of football? Is being a good bloke about mediocrity and averageness? If so, how can someone with the exceptional talents of Freddie Flintoff be seen to epitomise the idea?

And why won't we *ever* go to the bloody doctors?

WHAT IS A BLOKE?

I've already had a couple of tentative stabs, but let's try to properly define what a bloke is.

No one can agree where the word even came from. It was first recorded in 1851 by Henry Mayhew, the journalist who revealed the plight of London's poor to an indifferent Victorian nation. He said 'bloke' was replacing 'chap' as the preferred slang for any male, but the origin of that word is obscure. It could come from an Irish dialect word meaning 'likeable man'; it could also come from the Dutch word 'blok' which means 'fool', as in 'blockhead'. I think the modern meaning might fall somewhere between the two.

What a bloke definitely isn't is a 'geezer' or a 'lad'. To the untrained eye, they may appear the same but absolutely aren't. The word bloke is usually accompanied by an adjective prefix, which is often positive: 'decent' bloke, 'good' bloke, 'nice' bloke (although there is an unwritten law that if you want to tell the world a man makes you laugh then he is deemed to be a 'funny fella').

Geezers and lads don't get adjectives because their species is generally less complicated. Geezers and lads are the aardvarks and zebras of the male world: there are quite a lot of them, but they're easy to spot and narrow in range. Blokes are otters and apes, in that they're numerous, come in many different types and have a generally good temperament (so long as you don't steal their fish or bananas).

The bloke is also quintessentially British. Not as in wearing a top hat to work like Jacob Rees-Mogg or a kilt to weddings, like that half-Scottish bloke at work, but as in they don't really exist anywhere else in the world.

Germany may have *der Kerl*, Italy may be full of *ragazzi* and France can claim *le type*, but 'bloke' and all that implies belongs fully to these islands. I am willing to accept that Australia has a whiff of blokeyness about the place, but they're twenty years behind us so haven't fully developed yet (and that sort of comment, cheeky but basically affectionate, is classically blokey).

The bloke is also more emotionally complex than the alpha, geezer or lad. He is the dependable rank and file of the male species, the standard husband, father, uncle and brother who tries his best but doesn't have much agency in his own life (certainly when it comes to deciding how the house is decorated or what events will occupy the family calendar). It's a state of mind which usually occurs at a more senior stage of life, once you've had some of the headier dreams either kicked out of you or have willingly relinquished them for a quiet life. It's a mindset which descends once you've realised your main role isn't to thrust and conquer but to be a steady and dependable presence for those you love. And to carry heavy things. Blokes are inoffensive, pliable, dependable and calm, but also a bit shit at retaining any information about the people they're closest to.

A bloke knows the value of a pub quiz and the exact combination of alcohol and roast dinner which will result in a forty-minute nap. Though blokery is usually an older man's game, it's a mindset which could evolve at any age. I've had plenty of mates who were already wearing metaphorical cardigans and slippers during their GCSEs. I had a pal in Year 11 who brought a pack of biscuits to school with him every day and used to have a nap at breaktime. We didn't know whether to call him 'Hob Nob' or 'the cat', because he could sleep anywhere (on reflection, we should probably have advised him to get checked for diabetes).

Blokes are simple and yet some of our behaviour is so utterly daft and paradoxical you have to wonder if everything is as straightforward as it seems. It's tricky, though, because societally we're encouraged to think of blokes as basic creatures. For a long time, adverts have portrayed the woman as thrifty and resourceful, while the man was either confused, lazy or falling over in the background. In any sitcom you've ever seen, the dad is the comical figure. Why? Because he's a bloke and becoming a father in itself involves a fairly cataclysmic status drop.

We may be hard to define but there are certain things which characterise the British bloke.

One is that they're generally fairly content. Happy with just being. Give a bloke a dressing gown, some Twiglets and an obscure Bundesliga football match and he can sit happily for hours. He's genetically designed to find salvation in menial tasks. As children, boys will happily go to a beach only to ignore the majesty of the ocean or the beauty of the sunset and simply dig a hole. Even at that tender young age, he's just looking for a bit of peace and quiet.

If you see a man drinking a pint in an airport pub alone, that's a bloke. If you see a man driving to the tip on a Saturday morning with a smile on his face, that's a bloke. And if you see a man heading back from the tip and on the way to the pub, that's a very happy bloke.

The bloke doesn't like a fuss. The bloke is curious about the world and occasionally baffled by it. The bloke remains in touch with his inner child and retains a certain boyishness, which can be wrongly interpreted as immaturity.

Blokes will often suppress emotions, only for them to show up in the oddest of places. For example, it's OK to get a bit misty-eyed when watching *The Repair Shop*. The average bloke will be a tear-soaked mess as he watches a ninety-five-year-old woman collect the newly fixed clogs that her dead husband walked across Belgium in during the war. We tend to let our emotions out in massive bursts. We keep it all in, then binge on a big boxset of feelings. Whether that's when someone scores at the football, someone undertakes you on the motorway or when Blackadder asks his fellow soldiers to go over the top.

Blokes also have a tendency to be nostalgic – or rather, they don't so much yearn for the past as they want the future to slow down a bit and stop hurtling at them like a flying brick. Similarly, every bloke thinks that the younger generation has 'gone soft'. We'll forever lament the fact that young lads today can't even bleed a radiator or navigate without GPS. But my dad would despair that I couldn't change the oil on my own car and his great-grandad would despair that my dad bought meat in a butcher's rather than killed the animal with his bare hands.

The real bloke is *always* on the verge of giving up on modern football as each week brings further proof that the 'game is gone'. Luckily, he will never actually give up on modern football because, you know, his dad took him to his first game and he cherishes those smoky memories of angry beered-up men shouting sexual obscenities at the referee before leaving him outside a pub with a packet of crisps for three hours.

Despite how it sounds, these are happy memories. Like I keep saying about this whole bloke thing, it's a lot more complicated than it seems.

DO YOU WANT A MEDAL?

*British men do approximately half the amount
of housework of their female counterparts.*

It's fair to say that in modern heterosexual relationships, even
when the man and woman work the same number of hours,
women still do more of the housework. Many men have been
very happy for women to smash the glass ceiling, so long as they
didn't have to help clear up the mess.

How the hell have blokes blagged this continuing imbalance?
In a time when old boardroom dinosaurs are quaking and the
likes of Beyoncé have delivered finger-wagging rebukes to men
on all manner of behaviours, how have women increased their
workload outside the home but not experienced an equivalent
reduction within it?

There is one very simple reason, and it's possibly the hardest
to get past: most blokes are happier with lower levels of general
cleanliness.

I once lived in a lads' pad and it makes me shudder to think
about the state we'd let that flat fall into. One day, we decided to
have a party and it seemed, against all the odds, that there would
be actual girls present. We knew it was very unlikely they would
be getting off with any of us anyway, but especially not if the place
looked like a smackhead's bedroom.

I took the initiative and borrowed my mum's Dyson. Dysons

were new at the time and expensive, so my mum made me promise on pain of death to return it in the state it was lent.

We started vacuuming. The vacuum cleaner had completely filled up before we'd even done one quarter of the lounge (I won't burden you with what I saw in that despicable chamber, but the debris still pops up in anxiety dreams). It took another seven full loads before the Dyson, this shining evolution in cleaning, said 'fuck it' and conked out. The mess we had lived in for so many months had driven the high point of nineties British engineering to a spluttering death within half an hour.

I'd like to think I've evolved since then, that I'd avoid living in a public health hazard even if there weren't girls around – but the disparity between the mess me and my wife will put up with remains.

This lack of equality in housework isn't just confined to blokey blokes. Some of the most progressive men I know talk a good game on equality but deliver very little in domestic help. Sure, when they're on a company diversity retreat it's all 'this is what a feminist looks like' and echoing the idea that 'time's up' for out-of-touch men (in the hope that time won't be up for them), but ask them what a floor wipe looks like and they'll fumble around and mumble something positive about Caitlin Moran. On social media, they're the first to share memes saying men need to 'do better'. However, their feminism comes to a grinding halt when it comes to them 'doing better' in their own house and, in particular, cleaning the bathroom. I know a lot of blokes who do some household chores but it's very rare that any go near the bathroom. Or, indeed, are allowed near the bathroom. I guess women can live with half-hearted vacuuming, but a bad job in the bathroom could result in an outbreak of Legionnaire's disease. Weirdly, of the few blokes I know who do regularly clean the bathroom, most of them used to be in the army. That tells its own tale: all it took to instil this basic obligation was the possibility of a court martial.

I do some housework but, if I'm honest, I'm way too pleased with myself on the odd occasion that I do. This is going to piss some women off; however, I believe there can be no personal growth without full disclosure, so here comes a dangerous level of candour.

Whenever I do housework, in my mind, it counts as some sort of favour. [Winces in anticipation of blowback.] Rather than considering it a shared responsibility in the house we both live in, I see myself as a centre-forward tracking back to defend a corner and expect to be lauded to the rafters for entry-level teamwork.

I know it's not OK to think this way, but I also wonder if it might feel less like gaslighting to hear a bloke finally admit that this is how his mind works, when it's something many women will have suspected all along.

On the occasions I do housework, it will unfold in a similar way. It'll be on a day when I'm at home with less work to do than usual. In my sixth hour of watching something frivolous, like *The Mandalorian*, a thought will crop up in my head, seemingly out of nowhere: 'Geoff, you could vacuum the lounge.'

I'm initially taken with what a great guy I am for even thinking this. What a top bloke! So taken, in fact, that I almost forget to actually vacuum the lounge.

It's debatable as to whether I even do a good job of it because, for the duration of the work, I'm already anticipating my wife's return when I can share the good news.

The moment she puts her key in the door, I'm on her like a flash, barely allowing her time to put her coat on the hook before I relay my heroics.

'Babe, I vacuumed the lounge!' I proudly announce.

The look on my face must be like that of a three-year-old boy who finally did his first poo in the big toilet.

The reaction she gives is, I'd imagine, common to many women. 'What, Geoff? Do you want a medal?'

I laugh grandly, 'No, of course not – I just wanted you to know that I see this house as a shared enterprise and I'm just doing my bit and I shouldn't presume, and . . .'. I keep speaking but I'm guarding the pathetic truth that I do want a medal. I always want medals.

Men want medals. Is that so bad? This is mummy's little soldier you're talking to – as a boy, I was feted for the most limited acts of helpfulness by my indulgent mother so, yes, maybe the occasional medal wouldn't go amiss.

This is my advice to women whose blokes don't do enough housework, though I appreciate that they might not like it: purchase some medals. Go on eBay and get a job lot of cheap plastic ones, maybe a modest number to begin with, like a thousand.

Women might think, 'But why should I have to pander to his pathetic ego? He should want to empty the dishwasher.'

If he's young, there's a chance you could still train him, but be honest with yourself. Look into his eyes. Does he seem capable of change? Does he look like the kind of bloke who's ever going to 'want' to do a domestic chore when he could be watching golf? If the answer is no then follow my advice and your life will be better, albeit grudgingly.

Whenever he does a small task reward him, sometimes with more than one medal if he's done a particularly good job. Put a wash on? One medal. Took out bins without being reminded? Three medals. And if he notices that you've left that bottle of shampoo on the bottom step of the stairs in the hope he might take it up with him, give him the whole box.

FANCY A PINT?

Fancy. A. Pint.

For British blokes, this constitutes one of the greatest sentences in the English language. The 'To be or not to be' of blokery. And just like Hamlet's famous speech, the decision to have a pint can involve an aspect of moral quandary – not least 'Is 11am too early?'

But what is at the heart of this love affair with beer? Why is it so intrinsic to the blokey identity? Is it the drink itself or everything that goes with it?

Something I've always appreciated about beer is its longevity as a popular drink. In a world where every few months a new marketing campaign informs us we should be drinking espresso martinis, or something called a 'hard seltzer' (which sounds, to me, like over-the-counter medication for loose stools), the appeal of beer has endured. As far back as the Anglo-Saxon period, this country has been bang on the ale. In general, if something's been popular for that long it can't be all bad (though I say that conscious of the fact that bread had a fairly good run until the gluten-free evangelists mobilised).

Beer is a very simple drink, comprised of just four ingredients. Grain, hops, yeast and water. You can almost imagine a standard bloke at a bar crossing himself as he reverentially intones those four holy pillars: 'The grain, the hop, the barley . . . and a packet of pork scratchings please, love.'

Unlike many sugary or fizzy alcoholic drinks, a pint of beer – unless you're trying to win a bet or lose your dignity – is usually drunk at a slow, steady pace. The drink has various gravitating factors which hold you back. If you consume those gassy bubbles too quickly, you might get the hiccups or, worse still, find yourself staring into a toilet bowl. Given these restraints, the pint stands almost as a unit of time. An alcoholic hourglass. Or half-hour glass. Or fifteen-minute glass, if you've got a train to catch.

Speaking of trains, a pint can also act as a consolation. I believe it to be a fundamental British human right that when your train is cancelled or seriously delayed, you're entitled to get a bit drunk. It harnesses one of the standard functions of alcohol: drinking to forget (though admittedly I've sometimes also forgotten when the next train departs).

One key difference with other alcoholic drinks is the degree and speed at which beer dehydrates you. It depends on the ABV but the more sensible strength offerings won't dry you out as quickly as the likes of white wine and champagne. This allows longer periods of sustained drinking, hence why we have phrases like 'it's a good session lager'. No one in their right mind would think white wine is a shrewd 'session' anything. If you hunker down for a night on the Pinot Grigio you'll be crying or fighting much quicker. There's no beer equivalent to the phrase 'white wine werewolf'. Any of the changes in character which do occur from drinking beer tend to happen more gradually.

This is a selling point, especially for something like an all-dayer, which is like batting in a Test match. You have to think about tempo, intent and the crucial decision of when you first go for a piss. Even those toilet trips can be part of the ritual. The way women go for a pee means they're not familiar with standing next to someone else having their third leak in an hour and exchanging a good-humoured lamentation that they've prematurely 'broken the seal' (on the other hand, I've never known the bonding that goes with someone I've never met before giving me a tampon).

There's a nobility in being beer drunk. Any reckless muppet can sling eight shots of sambuca down their neck, but getting to the point where you're drunk on beer means you've managed your drinking time successfully. Breaks for spirits and mixers is cheating, though an old fashioned 'chaser' at the end of the night may be allowable (only if the urgency of 'last orders' has come into play). In that context, a chaser represents good time management, and you need to be suitably drunk to commence the tedium of getting home.

I realise I'm being very light-hearted about what is, after all, still an alcoholic drink. It can be tempting to paint beer as almost innocuous. There are plenty of blokes who don't even think having a beer is proper drinking. They may respond to the question of whether they're drunk by replying 'I've only had a few beers!', as though the nobility and longevity of beer somehow excuses them from the fact that they reek of ale and are stood in the garden eating yesterday's pizza straight from a bin.

The marketing lends itself to the idea of beer drinking as just a bit of fun and I've been deeply susceptible to all the big campaigns over the years. In my time, I've been Fosters guy and a Corona guy; I've drunk German beers, Czech beers and am currently dutifully consuming the widely marketed Italian brands a guy like me is supposed to enjoy.

But I've always been fascinated by the disparity between who actually drinks these lagers and the trendy types you see in their adverts – there's usually a big gulf between the two. Stella's marketing during the nineties was a prime example. The brand had a reputation as a very strong lager (with an even worse nickname) but their most memorable ad campaign depicted a struggling bohemian on his bike in rural France, stopping at a country pub and working in return for a pint of Stella and some artisan bread.

I've drunk Stella and eaten a French stick before, but it was standing alone in front of an open fridge at around 3am because I was spectacularly drunk.

The current trend is towards Italian lagers like Peroni and Moretti. The Moretti advert in particular is hilariously out of step with its core British market. We see young, sexy Italians, both male and female, enjoying a sensible Moretti or two. I'd say, at a push, most British blokes 'sensibly' enjoy the first two, after that it's anyone's guess. In fairness, advertising has to be aspirational; you can't have a commercial depicting a bloke my age sitting on a bar stool with a hand over one eye in a desperate bid to read the fifteen text messages from his wife. Nor could you show one of my mates outside a kebab shop pushing chips into his newly vacant head.

My reverence for beer hasn't always operated at its current level, but during the lockdowns being able to get a pint on draft was one of the few things I truly missed. Unlike drinks such as wine or spirits with mixers (where what you consume at home is identical to what you'd have in a pub), a draft lager is literally a different drink. And there's something about the artistry of pouring a pint which appeals to the blokey psyche. It's like a perfect golf swing or a flawless right hook. And, just like all fine art, it comes with jeopardy – mainly the mockery which can ensue when someone comes back with too much head on their pint and has to field hilarious queries as to whether he wants a 'flake in it'.

I'm not a Guinness drinker but I can understand how that drink runs even further with the artistry principle of pint pouring. There's something inexplicably beguiling about a smiling barmaid not only pulling a perfect pint but also including the pattern of a shamrock. Though some lads take the Irish connection too far, especially if they've decided you can only take your first sip facing in the general direction of Dublin.

During lockdown one, I heard a cruel rumour that some pubs were doing draft beer as carry-outs. I drove all around my area, only to find that this was either bollocks or not happening anywhere near me. It's the kind of disappointment I should keep to myself in later years when my son, whose formative childhood and schooling were fundamentally disrupted, asks me, 'Dad, what was your lowest moment during Covid?'

I'll solemnly claim it was the Delta variant but deep down the scars of several months drinking Stella exclusively from cans will still burn.

The beer you pour at home is never as good. For a start, you don't have the fancy pumps, some of which have gone from simple functionality to – in the case of Peroni – looking like an art installation by a steam-punk fanatic. Then there are the glasses. It's hard to get excited by a pint glass when it's marked by the familiar tideline of your dishwasher. The pub pint glass, however, is often branded and clean enough that it enhances that unique amber glow. A heavenly scene.

It wasn't the pouring alone which made me yearn for draft beer during those lockdowns, it was what the pouring suggested: that I was having a pint happily ensconced in a pub.

Pubs have, happily, become more accessible to women during my lifetime, but the standard features of what would still be seen as a traditional pub (beer on tap, dartboard, pool table, jukebox) suggest the grown-up version of a playground for men. And there's nothing blokes like more than growing up but staying the same.

There's also something character-building about simply walking into a pub. If you've got any sense, you'll fall into line with the general tone of the establishment. The ambience of each and every pub is its own 'house style', which if you enter disruptively you will unsettle. Going into a pub is a good exercise in adapting yourself to the needs of those around you. If you barge into a quiet pub noisily, you'll hear the unmistakeable chunter of a group of men who've all concluded you're a dickhead.

The appeal of having a pint endures. It's still the drink of choice for men in pretty much every region of Britain. This isn't just to do with those hoppy flavours.

As blokes, a lot of the social time we spend together is characterised by the incorporation of deliberate distractions. Whether we're watching sport on telly, sport in person or playing some kind of games console, the bloke often looks to factor in elements that mean we won't have to physically face each other for too long. Women don't seem to struggle as much with physical proximity. Have a look at two ladies meeting for coffee: they're often facing each other directly, shoulders almost mirror images of one another, their bodies inclined to denote full attention. For blokes, that kind of connectivity doesn't come so easy. Maybe my son's generation will arrive at a point where they can arrange themselves in front of their best mate and, from a distance of less than two yards, make full eye contact and ask, 'So, what's going on with *you*?' That kind of intimacy is some way off for blokes like me, but throw in the culturally understood disclaimer of a pint and we've got half a chance of sitting opposite one another for a time, a rare moment facing each other with our guards down.

And maybe there's something in those simple ingredients of beer, those four pillars. Something so simple and stable has obvious appeal for the average bloke. Maybe that's how he sees himself. Straightforward, uncomplicated and outside the fluctuating realms of faddy trends.

SOMETIMES YOU REALLY DO NEED TO 'MAN UP'

A few years ago, I saw an advert by Lloyds Bank which bugged me. It was a bunch of 'slebs' – no doubt being paid obscene amounts of money – who were queuing up to tell us why they hated the phrase 'man up'. It wasn't long after #MeToo and society had moved on to conducting a more general audit of the male psyche.

Watching the advert, I bristled. For one, I suspected a couple of the celebrities didn't fully believe what they were saying but had seen which way the cultural headwinds were blowing and elected to make a few quid off it. I was also suspicious of yet another big multinational riding the wave of whatever virtuous sentiment was doing the rounds that week. I have no idea whether the people who wrote, conceived of or indeed approved the ad believed 'man up' to be a genuinely harmful phrase. For all I know they could've signed off on the copy then gone on a debauched weekend in Prague firing rockets at cows. However, as we've all come to realise, corporations fear social media backlash above all else, so now we get lots of touchy-feely adverts which are the equivalent of that guy at college pretending to be a feminist so he could snog some girls.

For blokes, on a basic level, 'man up' is a useful shorthand for when you want another male to stop being fussy or simply take one for the team.

Picture a scenario: you're away on a stag-do; there's four of you in a budget hotel room. Three of the lads wish to sleep with a window open (for we are men, we *cannot* be too hot). However, your mate with the poor circulation doesn't stop wanging on about how cold it is. He's not going to win the argument, it's three against one, so eventually you just have to tell him to 'man up' and turn out the lights. There's no way you're all going to tolerate being hot just for him, plus the room needs a through breeze to dissipate the increasingly oppressive fog of man-musk.

Some people might take exception at the deployment of 'man up' in that context, but what else are we supposed to say?

'Come on Wayne, find your non-gender-specific inner fortitude!'

In such a scenario, I'm much happier to be a bloke. Simple democracy can win the day. I'd imagine the exact same scenario on a hen-do might play out a bit differently. Women, generally being more sensitive to other people's needs, might at the very least entertain soppy Claire who has suddenly declared she wishes to sleep with the light on. They know it's unworkable but they might talk through the issue, wishing to give nightmare Claire a sense that she's at least had her say. They might even explore the idea of the other three girls sleeping with blindfolds on. But I'd be hard pushed to sacrifice the simplicity of being able to tell another bloke to just belt up and crack on. It makes life easier for the tribe when you're able to play this card. Will Wayne have grown up nursing psychological traumas from being told to suck it up in this way? Possibly, but look at the upside: we as a society will spend less time sleeping in unnecessarily hot rooms.

And yet the phrase 'man up' is, in some quarters, *problematic* – possibly because there's an implied expectation that this characteristic is somehow exclusive to men. It's a fair point, especially given that the phrase involves the word 'man'. This doesn't, however, exclude women from having their own equivalent (though 'woman up' doesn't sound right . . .'Bird up'? . . .'Wench up'? It's hard to get a phrase that scans properly and doesn't sound like a sexist insult from the 1600s).

Women have plenty of words and expressions that celebrate qualities they think are unique to them. They can multitask. They can listen. They can clingfilm. They can actually find things in the house. Blokes rarely get upset when women claim all these virtues as their own.

There's even a song 'I'm Every Woman' (written by Nickolas Ashford and Valerie Simpson) which posits a litany of frankly supernatural abilities all women are believed to possess. The song incudes the belief that woman are mind readers who effectively manifest in the face of danger, then concludes with 'I ain't bragging'. No, not bragging at all. Just a clairvoyant oracle with the ability to physically appear in the face of peril and basically do everything.

But fair enough, it's a great song and only popular in the first place because women's emotional power is something we all benefit from and can identify.

But could you have a blokey equivalent of 'I'm Every Woman'? And what would it even sound like? Sadly, given the cultural tendency to think of blokes as rubbish, it would probably tend towards self-deprecation:

'I'm every geezer, it's all buried deep, deep within me.
I can't read your thoughts right now, nor do I have the inclination to.'

So, 'man up' has become a discredited phrase, even though 'balls' as a metaphor for courage has somehow continued largely uncontested. It's legitimate to query balls as a symbol of bravery because the metaphor actually correlates male biology with courage. But is it a myth?

Of the blokes I've known, the one with the biggest balls I've ever seen was a nervous wreck. Eventually he got the nickname 'Buster'. A lot of the women in our social circle got the wrong end of the stick and ended up discovering that his 'stick' wasn't the reason he was called 'Buster'.

Big balls, however, still carry with them the idea of prestige. Maybe this comes from the hokey idea that bigger testicles produce more sperm. Except it's not hokey at all: big bollocks really are more fertile (despite it seeming like one of those myths science would shrug off as bollocks). Some women prize large penises as a sign of virility, but the science suggests they should really be making potential suitors do a cough check rather than getting out the tape measure.

And what of this idea of courage coming from a man's balls? At the very least they do seem to produce more testosterone and are associated with higher levels of aggression – though aggression and bravery aren't the same thing (and as an owner of profoundly average-sized balls I would say that, right?).

One thing you can say about balls is that they're odd, the only delicate bodily organ to hang outside the body. It's a ridiculous design flaw to let something so vulnerable brave the elements in this way. That might be where the courage idea emanates from: it's not the balls which bestow bravery, it's the place they've chosen to live. Balls literally have the balls to be balls. They sit in full public view knowing they could get really cold, really hot or have a football slammed into them to the great delight of any watching males.

So I empathise a bit with queries over why balls stand as a metaphor for courage, but as society progresses in great leaps and bounds could we maybe just keep the idea that 'manning up' is a male thing? Call it 'heritage sexism'. The concept has uses we can all benefit from, especially when it comes to marshalling potentially unruly younger males.

Picture this: it's a family Christmas and you've invited too many people over (for many blokes, anything more than immediate family could be considered 'too many', but bear with me). You haven't got enough space to sleep everyone; you're a room and a blow-up mattress short. Someone in the family is going to have to sleep in the living room on a makeshift bed, made up of cushions from the couch. Who is going to take that bullet?

Definitely not Nanna.

Nor your uncle with the bad back.

Any of the middle-aged women? Nope, they won't have that.

The kids? It would feel too much like an adventure and they'd never stop talking.

So will it be the strapping twenty-five-year-old male family member?

Of *course* it will. He'll whine, sure, but you have a phrase at your disposal to eventually silence him: 'man up'. For this brief moment, he's expected to make a minor sacrifice for the good of the group.

Don't feel bad for him as he strops into the front room carrying the worst duvet in the house (often some god-awful floral relic from the seventies). This is a good moment for the lad, an opportunity for personal growth. He'll wear his morning backache as the equivalent of being daubed with blood after the first kill. He might make a fuss, but the reaction of the group will teach him that society does not care for a fussy man.

On a simple level, manning up is useful.

If the dogs need to be walked and it's raining – man up.

If the takeaway brought three Big Macs and one Filet-O-Fish, but no one really wanted the Filet-O-Fish – bloody man up and eat that fishy burger.

When a nervous flyer really wants the aisle seat but you desperately didn't want to sit in the middle so paid extra to avoid it, but this person is freaking out and, hey, it's just a twelve-hour flight, right? Man up. Sit in that seat. Everyone on the plane will benefit from you doing so, even if the large sleeping man next to you has started whimpering and nuzzling your shoulder.

There are obvious limits to 'manning up'. It is not applicable to anything in and around your actual physical health. Whatever the tough-guy gurus say, there are no viruses or cancers which can be 'sweated out'. And if being forced to sleep on couches is causing genuine mental health issues, say, if it's drifted into a sixth week, even when there are beds free, it's time to speak up.

Manning up isn't a gentleman-only club, everyone's welcome; it would just be nice if it was one phrase we could hold on to. Only time will tell. But for now, consider the merits of 'manning up', knocking your everyday sense of importance down a peg or two. Job done.

HEROES OF BLOKEDOM #1: FREDDIE FLINTOFF

Like many blokes, the summer of 2005 largely passed me by as I was fixated on the Ashes cricket series between England and Australia. It started in late July and before I knew it, I was unceremoniously dumped into early autumn, my mental bandwidth having been dominated for weeks by a titanic tussle between an ageing but still excellent Australian side and an England team coming to pre-eminence. Not only that, England hadn't beaten Australia for seventeen years.

We'd lost so heavily and often in the preceding years that watching England play Australia had become a process of self-flagellation, where small victories had to be treated like big ones. Unremarkable end-of-series dead rubber victories were practically celebrated with ticker-tape parades. Even one of our players scoring a quick fifty could feel like a solid case for a knighthood. Learning to love cricket during this dismal era set me up for a lifetime love of the sport. To bastardise a modern meme: 'If you don't love me at my worst, you don't deserve me at my nail-biting best.'

Standing above that epic series was the formidable figure of Andrew 'Freddie' Flintoff. In all the hero worship that followed it was almost forgotten his first name sounded vaguely middle class. He never *seemed* like an Andrew. The 'Freddie' moniker

24

was far more apt for what he represented to the general British public. It had the alliteration which always cements a name in your brain. One of my best mates is called 'Matt Marney'. Everyone remembers Matt, not least because he's a great bloke and a force of nature, but it's also fun to say his name. 'Do you know Matt Marney?' – it rolls off the tongue.

Meanwhile, 'Geoff Norcott' is a clunky stop-start affair which lacks any genuine cadence (the fact I was the second successive man in my family to go by that name is hard to fathom).

But when it came to 'Fred', everything was in place for him to climb straight into the nation's hearts and set up camp forever.

During that seesaw Ashes series, every time Australia started to re-assert their former dominance, Freddie stood up to them. Even in the first Test, though England ultimately lost that game, Fred slapped the Aussie bowlers to all parts during the second innings. At one point, he hit the ball so hard he broke his bat. Fred's own hardware couldn't stand up to the onslaught. It was like me, a comic, literally taking a roof off.

In the second Test, England had a better chance than usual as Australia's best fast bowler Glenn McGrath had stepped on a cricket ball while throwing a rugby ball around and was out injured (I'm ashamed to admit that upon hearing that news on the way to the ground I celebrated like I'd just won ten grand on a scratchcard).

England batted well in the first innings, but after a wobble we were threatening one of our trademark collapses. Freddie stepped to the Edgbaston crease and started heaving the ball around like he was trying to kill a pigeon in Wolverhampton. We scored 400 in a day, which doesn't sound like a lot amid the epic modern era of dizzying totals, but was it unheard of back then.

The Australian opening batsmen, Langer and Hayden, who I'd never seen take a backwards step, came out to bat a tricky few overs at the end of the day. However, they surprised us all by literally taking a backward step. There was only a light spot of rain in the air but those two pointed to the heavens like Noah trying to wrangle some free plywood. In days gone by, not only would tough Aussie males like them not have noticed the rain, for good measure they'd have wrestled a couple of crocodiles on their way to the middle.

The following day, with Australia rebuilding their innings, Aussie batsman Ricky Ponting was starting to look dangerous. Freddie came back on to bowl and had a couple of near misses. This seemed to be the way Ashes cricket had gone for so long, moments of English hope which eventually drift away, but Flintoff kept going and eventually got Ponting out with a peach (of a delivery . . . I'm aware most people reading this won't like cricket, bear with me).

This was the thing that didn't normally happen. Up to that point – before our nation actually started winning stuff – English sportsmen were past masters of the near miss. Whether it was losing on penalties or Tim Henman double faulting in a semi-final, we were all too familiar with the wry smile. Freddie actually prevailed. His smile was authentic.

English cricket has frequently served up all-action figures – before, in the shape of Ian Botham, and since, in figures such as Ben Stokes. But those two seem like men from another planet. Botham had a bit of eighties Hollywood glamour about him and Stokes has that otherworldly granite mentality of the modern elite performer. Fred, however, seemed ordinary in his extraordinariness. After England won that second Test by the barest of margins, while the other players were celebrating, he went over and crouched next to his crestfallen opponent Brett Lee to offer words of consolation. If that happened today I might go super-cynical and conclude that such a Corinthian gesture had been dreamed up by a team of sports image consultants, but given Freddie's temperament, it just felt like the natural action of a genuinely good bloke.

Even the way Flintoff celebrated England's series victory made him seem salt of the earth. He got drunk, very drunk, but crucially never acted like a dick. They say 'in vino veritas' and the fact that Flintoff could look like he fell asleep in a barrel of cider and still smile kindly suggested our hunches about his character were well founded. Yes, he pissed in the garden at Number Ten, but as blokey indiscretions go it could've been a lot worse. At least it wasn't in a sink. Or on the prime minister.

Growing up, every bloke knew someone a bit like Freddie – maybe not pound for pound in terms of actual ability, but someone who was ridiculously good at sport yet wore that talent lightly. Flintoff was one of those blokes who intuitively understood the relationship between man and ball. That seems to be the epitome of that kind of natural athlete – along with being good at everything else: the first time they pick up a ping-pong bat they play like a Chinese ten-time world champion. You'd think this would inspire envy but, in my experience, blokes tend to love a guy like this. In life, few are leaders; most of us are just looking for a guy to march behind.

I did eventually work in reasonably close proximity to the great man himself, writing for sports panel show *A League of their Own*. The first meeting was embarrassing. I played it super-cool . . . by reeling off a long list of stats from the 2004 South

Africa England series, speaking in rapid sporting clichés, and offering praise he must've heard a million times. This was all done in a breathless, nervous high pitch, like Kevin *and* Perry sped up and on helium. Freddie was very gracious – and when, on our second meeting, he remembered my first name I felt ten feet tall.

The standard idea is that blokes want to *be* their idols. I'm not sure that's entirely true. If I was Freddie Flintoff, who would be my Freddie Flintoff? Maybe that's Freddie's tragedy. For all his gifts of character and talent, unlike the rest of us, he doesn't have an Andrew Flintoff to look up to.

WHY WON'T MEN WEAR SUN CREAM?

On holiday, 82 per cent of women wear sun cream, versus only 65 per cent of men . . . who are probably acting under strict instruction.

SCENE

A family on holiday on the Costa Brava. It's 39 degrees centigrade. Grandpa looks lovingly at his daughter-in-law applying sunblock to his two beautiful grandchildren. She concludes the application.

> Keith: You missed a bit. Yeah that's right, get those little 'uns well and truly covered.
> Daughter-in-law: You should put some on, Keith. It's the middle of the day.
> Keith: Nah, not for me, love.

The daughter-in-law looks quizzically at Debbie, Keith's long-suffering wife. Debbie rolls her eyes at the younger woman; she's been trying to make Keith apply sun cream for the best part of forty years. She can't have this discussion again.

If your starting view of blokes is a dim one, you might pass off their reluctance to apply sun cream as simple idiocy or even laziness – the kind of short-sighted behaviour which helps ensure that men continue to die younger than women. It's easy to go with the simple explanation: blokes don't use sun cream because in the short term, it's easier to *not* use sun cream. There may well be future consequence to these actions but for now, they'll just . . . leave it. Perhaps that's it, pure laziness.

Or are they not applying sun cream because such an act of self-care identifies them as a bit limp? Scared? A bit 'girly'?

Or is it just straight-up bravado?

I've thought long and hard about this and have concluded that it's none of these. The truth is much more interesting.

Until not too long ago, in terms of our relative progress as a species, men were expected to go out and hunt. To do this, they had to withstand discomfort for the good of the tribe. They literally had to 'man up' or people might not get fed.

Now, I often casually quote our more primitive past as a way of explaining male behaviour, but it can also offer too easy an answer. It should also be said that – as much as I suspect hunter-gatherer instincts still echo down our DNA – I don't think I personally would have been a very useful man during that time. I'd have been a shit hunter.

People forget the 'gatherer' part of that equation. I suspect my family would've been doing a lot of gathering. In all likelihood, I'd have rocked up back at our shoddily built hut after several weeks 'hunting' sporting only a single rabbit, whose foul stench suggested it was already long dead by the time I accidentally stepped on it. And the suspicion would linger that I'd actually used the hunting expedition as a cover for getting some peace and quiet. The Stone Age equivalent of a salesman taking a motorway Travelodge even though the 'business trip' was only fourteen miles from home. When they excavated our settlement thousands of years later and examined our fossilised shit, my family's reliance on gathered nuts and berries would have been so great they'd have dubbed us 'the muesli people'.

But, despite my likely Stone Age incompetence, I still wonder if these hunter behaviours still reside in blokes somewhere, only to pop up thousands of years later on a beach in the Costa Brava. Once upon a time, while out hunting, it would've been important to demonstrate you weren't too precious about your own personal welfare. When stalking a yak, it wouldn't have instilled much confidence in the other males if you started bleating about a nettle sting. Or got the lads looking for pumice stones because the hard skin on your feet was getting out of hand. Perhaps knocking back the offer of sun cream is one of the last remaining options the modern bloke has to demonstrate his resilience.

Nowadays, as with many aspects of modern masculinity, not applying sun screen lacks the heroic sense of self-sacrifice you might have got from toughing it out on a hunting trip. Today, there's no glory left, no sucking it up for the good of the tribe, just you thinking you can tough out the unremitting glare of the hottest thing in our solar system. For a bit, anyway, until, on day five, you give in like a sulky teenager after your third bout of sunstroke.

If my generation are hard work, the familiar stubborn grandpa at the top of the chapter represents even more of a problem. Many women make the mistake of thinking they can inform older blokes about the risks of skin cancer and that information alone will change their behaviour. It's not that simple. In the same way people who've stuck with smoking ignore the gory modern packaging of cigarettes, any man who's got to sixty thinking his body has a unique ability to withstand the radiation of the *actual sun* is unlikely to change his ways. He'd have to admit that other things he left unattended might be a problem too, like his bad back or the fact he never got a hug off his dad.

My own dad wasn't one for sun cream. He wasn't one for hugging either. It's not that he was without empathy, but he could be hilariously blunt. My parents were already long divorced by the time my mother died in 2009. My dad had been relatively attentive in the immediate aftermath of her passing. He'd checked in more often than not and was making a special effort to not remind me of other comedians with more successful careers.

About six months after she'd gone, I was a little late to meet up with him (he hated lateness above all else; he'd have rather I'd done a degree in dance and movement). He asked me where I'd been. I told him I'd been at a counselling session which had over-run.

He furrowed his brow. 'Counselling? Are you still doing all *that*?'

For once, I responded as a comedian rather than as a son. 'Well she's still dead, ain't she?'

Dad paid for lunch that day.

He wasn't one for therapy himself, just as he wasn't one for sunblock. The aversion comes from exactly the same well. That kind of self-preservation would just never occur to him. To preserve the self is to admit vulnerability.

Part of the sunblock aversion could also come down to the physical embarrassment of having to apply it. Blokes may deem the process of putting on suntan lotion to be a weird act of public self-love. In general, men aren't well versed in the maintenance of their own bodies full stop, let alone on a beach. I remember the reproachful look my dad gave me when he found out I used moisturiser on my face. I had to hold off letting him know that I'd bought a man-bag – there was only so much subversion he could handle in one day.

It's not just the perceived vanity of applying sunblock which poses a problem, it's the competence. Have you *seen* a bloke applying suntan lotion? They do it with the same conviction most men display clingfilming leftovers for the fridge. It's obvious most of us have never contemplated how to navigate that tricky bit of our middle back. There's a lack of match experience and we end up looking like cats when they sacrifice their dignity to lick that awkward spot between neck and chin.

Rather than trying to smoothly and evenly distribute the cream on their body, blokes get frustrated and resort to effectively slapping themselves across the chest and back – like a weird form of tub-thumping. It's simply not possible for them to dissociate the idea that applying any cream to the body is something women do.

So the sun cream dilemma serves as a good example for the sometimes bewildering nature of the bloke's conduct. On the face of it, there's belligerence and stubbornness, but those are the symptoms rather than the condition. The behaviour is driven by huge sliding tectonic plates of masculinity. People would rather deal with the surface level actions than acknowledge that masculinity is confusing – so confusing, in fact, that it's often easier to present it as basic.

So when you see one of us decline sunblock in forty-degree heat, it might not just be laziness or bravado, it's more likely to be an anxious, deeply felt instinct which also helps keep a lid on a whole can of psychological man-worms.

JOEY DOESN'T SHARE FOOD!

In the sitcom *Friends*, part of the appeal of the character Joey Tribbiani lay in his consummate representation of the typical bloke – the American version, but one which clearly resonated with a British audience. Joey liked sport, girls and – most importantly – food. He represented male simplicity in its most basic and loveable form.

Whenever he exhibited predictable blokey behaviours for a punchline I was always surprised by the degree to which some women in the live studio audience would offer up a whoop of endorsement. There was something about his basic manliness they approved of. Though it's highly probable that those quasi-primitive behaviours came across as sexy because the actor perpetrating them was, himself, very sexy. Eating a massive pizza by yourself is significantly less endearing when you don't look like Matt LeBlanc did in the early noughties.

The whoops were never louder than when Joey would eat voraciously. Whether it was food off the floor, food no one else wanted or sandwiches stashed in comical places, there's something about having a good appetite which seems undeniably manly.

When you're dating a woman and eat with her family for the first time there's a curious unspoken obligation that you will eat well, preferably taking in a fair portion of meat. If you're being cooked for at the family home, there's a further expectation that you will honour the chef, meaning that if you don't go for a second or, preferably, third helping, there could be furtive glances between her relatives.

Who is this man you've brought to us? Is he rude? Weak? A VEGAN???

However, if you complete a third helping – or if in a restaurant, order the biggest steak and make light work of it – you'll most likely get a pat on the back and this healthy first outing will reassure the family unit that you're not a weirdo.

The need to eat heartily diminishes once they learn to trust you, but if you become part of the family, be warned – this expectation has a habit of coming back into play, especially around festive meals.

One year, I had a third helping of Christmas dinner. This became a talking point and I realised I'd essentially done what cricket umpires do when they take a light reading as to whether it's too dark to continue play: I'd set a standard of three helpings. 'Old Geoffrey Three Helpings!' But I'm now in my mid-forties and if old Geoffrey Three Helpings continued on his roguish big-appetited path, their hope I'd put in a good shift at the dinner table may eventually be trumped by concerns that my wife had married someone with an emerging co-morbidity.

To get around this, I've had to come up with strategies to sustain this reputation without dying from high cholesterol. So here are my tips.

1. For some reason, no one really clocks how much food you're having on your first helping, so make sure you hit all the main food groups but keep it modest.

2. Get up quickly for helping two. This identifies you as a good appetite guy. 'What's he *like*?' they'll all say indulgently. However, this is where the strategy element comes in. On this helping you have more of what you skimped on in the first, but no meat this time. A couple of potatoes and loads of veg. A packed plate but not a mental number of calories.

3. The third helping is the showstopper. You want to wait until the other men are flagging, sitting back and tapping their paunches, as if food is a form of wrestling and they're happy to submit. Then, you stand up again with your plate (in my mind this is all done in slo-mo, possibly to the theme from *Gladiator*). This time you go big on the meat and – yes – another Yorkshire. A man who likes meat and Yorkshires can't be all bad. Enjoy the high fives on the way back to your seat, knowing that when you fall asleep in roughly forty minutes it's because you did God's work.

There's no obvious logic for the cultural expectation that blokes will go big at family meals. We know that men's bodies are on average larger and therefore require a higher daily calorific intake. But in a time of increasing sensitivity around women's body shapes and of equality between the genders, many restaurants and food outlets have gone for the broader idea of 2,000 daily calories for adults. But implying that men and women need the same amount of calories isn't scientific. It's like claiming you'd need as much petrol to fill up a Range Rover as you would a Kia Ceed (no shade on women; to me, the Ceed, with it's incredible MPG and warranty, represents the superior vehicle).

It seems odd to ignore the effect biology would play on your calorific needs, but it could be a reflection of a trend where many modern men find themselves in less physical jobs. These days, Derek in finance probably doesn't need his sausage baguette to be one third bigger than Pauline's in HR, because he spends exactly as much time sitting on his arse as she does.

Hunger does seem to be more of an immediate driving force for blokes though. If I think about the people I know who suffer most acutely from the 'hanger' phenomenon (the idea that some people *have* to satisfy their hunger immediately or will start throwing cutlery around), it's pretty much exclusively blokes.

I have a window of about twenty minutes from first hunger pangs to thinking I'll expire on the spot if I don't neck an emergency lump of cheese. This disposition can create anxiety, particularly when dining at restaurants.

One of my big issues with restaurants is that I'm not in control of when I'm going to eat. A lot of Turkish places cover this by immediately bringing out bread and olives. That's pretty much an automatic five-star rating from me. Even if the subsequent chicken kebab contained feather and beak, I'd still award no less than a four. Immediate bread means you can relax, settle into the environment and think about what to order with a clear head.

Otherwise, there's a lot of waiting. First for the waiter to come to the table. Even when they turn up, they might cockily (in my mind anyway) inform you that they're only doing drinks orders first. I'd have hoped the fact I was chewing the place mats was a clue I was good to go.

You might then find yourself in the situation where – when the waiter eventually deigns to come for the food order – someone in the group will grandly announce, 'Oh, we haven't even *looked* at the menu yet!' As though we're all devastating raconteurs rather than disorganised muppets who haven't made a single attempt at addressing the primary reason we're there in the first place. Then I start to fret that, having been dismissed in this off-hand manner, the waiter may never return. Ever. (It could be hanger, or something I should talk to my counsellor about.)

It can be tempting to think that men are the sex who are all about the food. We have sayings which support this idea, such as, 'The way to a man's heart is through his stomach.' But have you ever cooked a woman a good meal? They seem pretty happy about it. When blokes do eat it's often with a grim sense of duty. I've always admired the steely commitment workmen exhibit in greasy-spoon cafés as they try to cram so many food groups onto a fork that it seems like an attempt at a weird world record.

I'm not sure blokes do enjoy food more than women, but I do think we're wired to think we should 'feast' differently. In many cultures, a man who eats well sets others at ease. Like so many other things, just do it, whether you want to or not. It's just another peculiar aspect of being a bloke.

'I'm not a smart man,
but I know what love is.'

Forrest Gump

BLOKEY FILM REVISIONS #1:
JERRY MAGUIRE

In the spectrum of your life as a male, middle age represents a unique vantage point where you're still just about in touch with the boy you once were but also staring out to the horizon of the old bastard you'll soon become. I've noticed that in my own sweet spot of blokedom I've started to rewatch classic films through a slightly different lens.

When I first saw *Jerry Maguire* I simply thought it was a very good film. It had Tom Cruise (always a good start), Cuba Gooding Jr on objectively hilarious form, Renée Zellweger being lovely, and that little blonde kid being so cute I never want to see a clickbait link saying 'Do you know what the kid from Jerry Maguire looks like now?' (If it turns out that pure-faced boy eventually became a crackhead I too shall hit the pipe.)

Jerry Maguire is one of those glossy agreeable films of the mid-nineties which – even if people don't love – they rarely have anything against. Recently, as I've become more of a film buff, I've tried to work out what genre it falls into.

It's definitely not an action film, though being a Tom Cruise movie there is of course a bit where he sprints for no apparent reason.

It's funny but not explicitly a comedy – certainly not whenever Cuba is absent from a scene.

Is it a sports movie? Kind of. It does tell the tale of a jobbing pro waiting for his moment in the sun, but that doesn't form enough of a central narrative to rank alongside films like *The Way Back*, *Rocky* or *King Richard*.

Then it hit me: *Jerry Maguire* is a romcom for blokes. It's pretty much a one-movie genre.

I'm not saying that prior to *Jerry Maguire* I hadn't also enjoyed romcoms principally aimed at women. Like many blokes, I sometimes protest too much when we settle down to *Maid in Manhattan* or *Sleepless in Seattle*, only to mysteriously develop a dust allergy during the final act. However, I reserve the right to mock all the obvious tropes, such as the kooky woman with her own cottage industry who meets a handsome billionaire yet *somehow* finds a way to love him. Or the bloke making an over-the-top romantic gesture to a woman he hardly knows. Even the fact that these movies almost always suggest that opposites attract (I'd say, particularly over the last few years, that opposites repel, certainly if Brexit comes up).

Then there's the cliché of couples snogging in the rain (I don't want to stereotype . . . well, evidently I do . . . but in the real world, women and rain don't go well together – what Spiderman can do upside down in the pissing rain would have most women dashing to take cover under the entrance to Argos).

Some recent feminist discourse has made certain generic features of romcoms a little trickier to pull off. For example, persistence was always a guaranteed winner for our male romantic lead, but now there's a fine line between showing an interest and showing up at her flat unannounced (again). Previously, the leading man would usually have personality traits that would challenge the leading lady: *So you're against big corporations . . . but remind me of your favourite coffee chain?* As we all know, a man who calls out a woman's low-level hypocrisies within minutes of meeting her is guaranteed to get a shag.

Even the ubiquitous mad dash to the airport is replete with modern pitfalls. If you were somehow able to crunch the usual two hours of security into a few minutes, you'd probably emerge with some Just Stop Oil protestor superglued to your leg. And if you did finally get within six feet of the stunned woman you'd be Tasered as a potential terrorist or sex pest.

So generic romcoms have become harder to pull off, but what *Jerry Maguire* did was something I hadn't seen done before or since: it articulated a common romantic fantasy of many men.

To begin with, Jerry has it all. So he's proved he can be a basic millionaire, no sweat, but he then has an attack of conscience. He doesn't just want to be rich; he wants to be rich the *right* way. At his high point of moral grandstanding, Jerry is dumped on his arse by a sports representation agency. The only person who stands by him is the impossibly lovely Dorothy who, despite being a single mum, walks out on a good job to go into business with a deranged man holding a goldfish.

In fairness to the film, it addresses the plausibility issues through Dorothy's funny yet cynical sister, but nevertheless, the plot rolls on and Jerry – in one of those mad moments of romantic mania every bloke has at least once in his life – declares that the couple should set up home together. He likes Dorothy but loves her son (who wouldn't? I would happily spend six years in a loveless marriage just to play catch with that kid).

This is a revolutionary storyline. We have a man who actively wants to be a stepfather; he feels a greater draw to that role than to romantic love. We come to realise, however, that the barrier between Jerry and Dorothy isn't that he doesn't love her, it's that he doesn't feel enough of a man to be what she needs. He's not worthy of her love. Not yet, anyway.

This is a shrewd direction for the film to go in because men can feel that their living defines them in the eyes of their other half. Whenever a bloke becomes jobless, his functional worth is judged more harshly. I've known several men get made redundant in middle age and one of the things they always wonder in their darker moments is 'Will she leave me?'

Do women have this thought when they get made redundant or fired? I honestly don't know, but it would be a very odd development in a friendship group if a woman reported that, after just six months out of work, the bloke kicked her out: 'I can't believe it, girls; he kept singing you've got to have a j-o-b if you wanna be with me. Apparently, the only thing *going on* was the rent.'

For blokes, from the moment you get your first full-time job, often aged around nineteen to twenty-one, you're expected to aim for roughly forty-five years of unbroken employment. Statistically, you might spend some time out of the workforce, but the general expectation is that may amount to only a year or two of your entire adult life. Staying employed for such a large portion of your life is a tall order and the necessity to earn can become the mother of all invention, but it can also manifest in anxiety dreams in which you're the least well-endowed bloke in *The Full Monty*.

Jerry Maguire works as a romcom because it offers a world

where everything can go horribly wrong at a crucial point in your professional life, but with a best friend who sticks by you through thick and thin, a good woman by your side, and an impossibly cute stepson, you can still find a way to be the man you want to be and the man they need.

That's why, for blokes, *Jerry Maguire* is a groundbreaking movie and a truly romantic ideal.

YOU LOOK SMART

A lot of blokes resent the obligation to dress smartly for formal social events because, broadly speaking, we don't like 'dressing up'.

It's the cause of frustration in many relationships and the process of encouraging a man to 'make an effort' is a negotiation which may start months before the actual event. There are some blokes who will push this to the limit and try to wear a T-shirt, sometimes even flipflops, to a wedding – but most of us tend to close the deal some way nearer to what our other half wants.

It's almost always the smarter move.

I have a lifelong aversion to wearing smart clothes. I don't just dislike it, I actively resent it. Whenever I'm expected to wear a suit, tie or a shirt for any occasion, I'm transported back in time, and I'm once again that little boy who was reluctantly having a brutal side-parting combed into his hair by an intent mother. Even today, as I do up a tie, I can feel the freshly salivaed thumb of senior women in my family smudging away marks on my face, like their spit was nature's anti-bacterial wipe.

When I was a teacher I did wear a suit to work, but that was only because I'd worked out that teenagers are incredibly superficial creatures and – for some weird reason – dressing like

I was from 1980s Special Branch made it marginally less likely that the pupils would stab each other with a compass.

I feel bad about this churlishness around wearing formal attire. I'm aware that my wife and many women feel great scrutiny towards their appearance at big social occasions. I've seen the stress it puts on my wife, particularly on the occasions when we've headed to an overseas wedding and our bag has been last out at baggage reclaim. I'm also conscious that I'm delving into some fairly stereotypical comments about gender and weddings, that men grudgingly fall into line while women fret about how they look.

In my defence, weddings, by definition, are incredibly gender stereotypical.

Weddings are a ritual almost exclusively based on presumptive and old-fashioned ideas about the two sexes. Yes, we tinker – sometimes the bride is 'given away' by a woman and many modern brides make speeches – but the whole day is dripping with heteronormativity (which might be why every gay wedding I've ever attended was over-subscribed).

No matter what kind of wedding it is, the pressure on women to look good is palpable. Men are expected to look 'presentable', which doesn't carry the same weight of expectation. However, there is a flipside to this: if a woman nails her look on a big day, she'll spend the whole event being told how lovely she looks. Not just that, if she *really* nails it, in years to come, female friends and relatives will literally remember what she wore.

'Oh my God, that white jumpsuit!'

'The one with the straps?' another friend will chime in.

'Amazing,' the third will conclude.

I don't need to understand why women are able to remember

other people's clothing in such detail. Equally, I can't explain why I don't remember the place settings at my own wedding but am able to tell you that Wimbledon FC's goalkeeper at the beginning of the 1988–89 season was Simon Tracey. We all have our own mysteries and at least women's recall tends to be reserved for things they were actively involved in.

So I think part of the reason women put effort into their appearances on big occasions is because they know the rewards are there. The stakes just aren't the same for blokes. The top-end outcome for us is that someone will give you a cursory up and down look then say 'Don't you look smart?' (which is not even a full compliment but a rhetorical one). Maybe they've clocked that it's the same suit you wear to weddings, funerals and the occasional job interview. Forget the fact you lost weight for the wedding or that you re-did your side parting three times (three!). Nope, it's 'You look smart'. The same compliment you get right from being that reluctant eight-year-old boy up to being a fully grown man – because God forbid you pull focus from the shimmering princess by your side.

And it's fair; you put in the hours, you get the rewards. Since make-up hasn't yet become part of mainstream male culture, we don't have the tools at our disposal to attract attention in the same way. I'm glad. Make-up would do my head in. It's a time-consuming ritual which I'm grateful most blokes aren't routinely expected to engage in.

Whoever that first woman to decorate her face was, she changed the game forever. I often picture that initial sliding-doors moment when a woman applied something to her face to enhance her attractiveness. In some prehistoric time, a woman – let's call her 'Danielle' – was out tilling the fields when she accidentally pricked her finger. She noticed a small bead of bright red blood at the tip of her index finger. In a moment of inspiration, she applied it to her lips. Immediately, she got more attention from the basic and predictable males around her, who made approving noises which roughly translated as 'Ugh, same woman look slightly different'.

I picture how the wiser women in the tribe would've reacted to this seismic development, leaning against a tree, thinking, 'You silly cow, Danielle. Do you know what you've started? You've basically instigated the beauty equivalent of a nuclear arms race in which whatever one woman does other women will have to match or exceed it. Just know that one day in thousands of years, some women will feel obliged to get up earlier than their families to paint their faces because they don't want to be judged at the school gate.'

If men do want to stand out we could take bolder choices with our outfits. At one friend's wedding – under my wife's sage advice – I wore a flamboyant pink shirt and got a lot of praise . . . actually she's just reminded me it was 'hot pink', and maybe this is part of the problem.

Blokes literally don't see the same colour spectrum women do. After twenty years of marriage, I'm convinced that women don't actually believe in the existence of the colour black. No matter how certain you are that something is black, they'll be on hand to casually correct you that it is in fact 'midnight blue'.

It turns out this is one of those biology issues; women are literally more capable when it comes to correctly assessing a colour and can detect more shades than men. That's why advertising for the Dulux colour scheme targets women, usually showing a woman on a couch protectively hugging a mug in a beautiful and recently decorated purple living room. Sorry, 'mauve'.

The different pressure on women to look good is something blokes have to just accept. I see it at close hand via my female colleagues on TV. They undergo much greater scrutiny than male comedians. Similarly, just like weddings, they also tend to get a lot more praise, to the point where they can get free clothes off the designers. I have never had a panel show appearance go out and been tweeted, 'Dude, where *did* you get that faded polo shirt?'

My son has been clever enough to remember the attention he's got for wearing a smart waistcoat or a natty hat. Where I once wriggled as my mum dressed me, he happily submits to the process because he trusts my wife's judgement. I'm sometimes envious of how sharp he looks and the praise he gets. Given our physical similarities, they are often outfits which might look alright on me too. This isn't a coincidence; I think my wife has given up trying to make me more stylish and is instead focusing her energies on him.

Me? I'm too basic and long in the tooth to become stylish. As long as I've shaved, I smell alright and am wearing matching socks, I reckon I'll be fine in polite society. I'm in my mid-forties for God's sake. When it comes to big family events, I'll take a perfunctory 'You look smart' if it means I can spend another hour watching *Soccer Saturday*, safely detached from the chaos and army of hair straighteners upstairs.

MEN'S INTUITION

More than half of British men gamble.

Throughout history, there have been a fair number of blokes who believe they can predict the future. Sometimes it's fellas like Nostradamus prophesising the end of humanity; sometimes it's politicians making ominous speeches, and sometimes it's just your dad's mate spending all day down the bookies because he thinks he can work out who has the fastest dog.

This last example represents the most common form of male soothsaying: gambling.

For most blokes, the occasional bit of gambling is a measured pastime. However, they'll often harbour the daydream that they could take it further, and talk in hushed, reverential tones of a bloke they knew who 'actually made a living by gambling'.

The need to believe in this mythical individual speaks to a particular fantasy that not only can you win the occasional cheeky twenty quid here and there, you can actually monetise your unique talent for watching sport. I'm not saying there haven't been men who have gambled and done OK – for a while – but we tend to mysteriously leave their story at the point they won thirty grand at Cheltenham, not two years later when they were selling their kid's Xbox at Cash Converters.

Serious gambling is something I'm grateful not to have the gene for. Not only do I not have it in my blood; I just don't *get* what that buzz is. I've had plenty of friends who do, but how they get their kicks has always perplexed me.

I spent a day at Cheltenham Races with one mate who 'likes to put a bet on' (a classic blokey understatement, in the same way that 'he can handle himself' usually means 'he's a violent psychopath'). He had a good day at the racecourse and won around three grand. As we were travelling back into town to start the evening's drinking, thereby moving the gambling instinct to betting on the capacity of our livers, he was checking his phone for local casinos.

I spoke to him a few days after that and asked why he'd eventually left a great night out to carry on gambling (and ultimately lose most of his winnings, it turned out). He said it was because he was chasing the rush.

But what was the 'rush' like? I didn't understand.

He explained, 'You know when you're driving and the car in front suddenly comes to a halt and you have to slam on the brakes?'

I nodded and waited.

He gestured with his hands as if to say, 'Voila! There's your buzz.'

I replied, 'That's a horrible feeling.'

He looked a bit rueful then said, 'Well, we all gamble on something.'

As a pursuit, hobby or addiction, gambling has changed a lot in my lifetime. Blokes of my vintage and above will remember the bookmakers of the eighties and early nineties: a bunch of – often – seedy-looking geezers, standing together but not together, smoking roll-ups and staring at screens. It was like a pub without the pork scratchings or the occasional sound of laughter.

Eventually, in the same way that people who ran football realised how off-putting the environment felt to women, bookmakers realised they might be leaving money on the table, what with half the population viewing entering a betting shop as being akin to walking down by the docks alone late at night. In came cleaner, well-lit bookies, with pastel shades and a welcome reduction in the general sense of sadness. I wouldn't say nipping along to the bookies has become a standard activity for most women, but it's now something they could do without feeling like they need a bodyguard.

My mum gambled, but her version tended to take place in the bingo hall. She made the smart move of calling her weekly trip 'having a flutter'. I went with her a couple of times and all her bingo buddies claimed it was the social element they craved, but once the caller started they had their dabbers brandished like weapons and stared daggers at whichever lucky cow called 'haaase' ahead of them.

The real revolution in gambling over the last fifteen years has been the online sphere. This industry has evolved to hook young men with devastating efficiency. Adverts depict impossibly handsome men, dressed like descendants of the Peaky Blinders, checking their phones while inevitably accompanied by a WAG-style trophy blonde.

Female online gambling in the form of sites like Foxy Bingo has been on the rise too. Overall participation in some form of gambling runs nearly at fifty-fifty these days, but the percentage of people who go on to become compulsive and form addictions are overwhelmingly men.

One such innovation, which was always going to be catnip to blokes, is 'cashing out', where the gambler gets to feel like Gordon Gekko, holding his nerve on deals which could make millions, as opposed to Gordon from Telford, deciding whether to take £25 winnings because Swindon have just taken the lead against Newport County.

The genius of the bookmaker's marketing is to play to the male tendency to fantasise. If they're not trying to make you think you're Tommy Shelby crossed with Jeff Bezos, the other way gambling markets itself is by suggesting that betting is akin to involvement in the sport itself.

For a while, Sky Bet ran a campaign saying, 'It matters more when there's money on it.' No shit. Everything matters more when there's money involved. Gambling, divorces – your relationships with family as they read out the will. They were trying to encourage men to find a new level of sporting meaning by leveraging their own finances.

Typically, no one would care too much about a midweek Papa John's trophy game between Portsmouth and Leyton Orient, but stick twenty quid on it ending nil–nil in normal time and *you're practically in the dug-out* (if Ray Winstone uses that slogan I will sue for royalties).

I suspect this strategy plays to the sense of wonderment at sport which many men felt in their younger years but lost as they grew older. As you age and other commitments compete for your attention, it gets harder to zero in to the same degree . . . *unless* you put money on it. If there's money involved you're believing in sport Santa again, like a thirty-year-old leaving out reindeer food in a tenth-floor flat.

Gambling addiction is a serious affliction and the online

arena does seem to have opened up new and creative ways for blokes to lose their shirts. For most of us, however, sticking the odd bet on remains a sensibly managed pastime.

The majority of my mates bet sensibly and tend to go small on something like an accumulator. They put down anything from £5 to £20 trying to predict numerous results where the odds are similarly multiplied and they could walk away with several thousand pounds.

It seems simple on paper. You pick a bunch of the odds-on favourites but bring your blokey sporting intuition to bear as you stick an unlikely 'x' by Middlesbrough for an away win. The other mortal males would never dream of backing 'Brough that weekend, but *you* have contacts (and by 'contacts' I mean you were listening to a football podcast with Micah Richards and found out their keeper has finally shaken off that troublesome wrist injury).

Pretty much no one ever wins on the big football accumulators, in the same way that no one ever wins that luxury sports car being raffled in an airport departure lounge. The footie accumulator bloke will, nevertheless, still share stories of his near misses like glorious tales of war. If it hadn't been for that last-minute equaliser by York City in the Vanarama National League he'd be a millionaire (Rodders), but the reason the odds are so long is because, in a series of ten bets, those unlikely twists are factored in. Bookmakers don't become millionaires by not knowing that, sometimes, a team of absolute donkeys might shin one into the net during the last minute of injury time.

Maybe the accumulator bloke doesn't ever want or expect to win. The real story is in the close shaves, the last-minute penalties which robbed them of that early retirement in Marbs.

At least society has a long-standing understanding of men who like to gamble. The more recent crypto phenomenon is a lot less well established and even more confusing. The crypto guy is way more tedious than the bloke posting photos of his betting slip on social media. The crypto guy is willing to invest in pretend money then spend the next six years of his life monitoring that one billionth of a Bitcoin like a male penguin nursing an egg.

It's not to say there won't be blokes who do well out of crypto, but it's unlikely to be you. My view has always been that if they're advertising to schmucks like me, the big ship has probably already sailed.

Gambling speaks to an innate sense in many blokes that we want, and sometimes need, to take risks.

Perhaps the gambling impulse is a deeper manifestation of the two sexes' relationship with the past, present and future. The phenomenon of women's intuition suggests that they fancy themselves as shrewd readers of everything that's happened before. The equivalent delusion men suffer from is the idea that they can predict everything that will happen from this point on. Maybe not floods, house prices, or even whether she'll stay with you once the kids leave home – but we do fancy ourselves to call the correct score in the upcoming Ashes series.

Gambling is and always will be a mug's game. If you need further evidence, look no further than the vibrant betting markets in and around Kim Jong Un. There are all sorts of things you can bet on regarding the North Korean dictator: when he'll leave office, how he'll leave office, when he'll die and – at one point – whether or not he would play a round of golf with the then US president, Donald Trump.

What kind of psychopath bets on the next move of a psychopath?

If you're STILL not convinced gambling's a mug's game, Paddy Power has in the past offered odds on when the world would end. If you were correct, and your estimation beat the expectations of every single respectable scientist, how the hell do you propose to collect your winnings?

Maybe the winnings aren't the point. Maybe it's getting to proudly text your mate a picture of your betting slip just before a giant meteor slams into the earth, with the caption 'Called it!'. There's no way of checking, but I'd guess every single person who has bet on the date of the world ending was a bloke. There wouldn't be too many women in their right mind who would bet on something so ridiculous.

Britain's richest woman is, after all, a bookmaker, which says it all.

PINK JOBS, BLUE JOBS

In the 2017 general election, then prime minister Theresa May gave a notorious interview (in fact she gave several during that campaign, but this is the one which didn't involve running through grass).

In an attempt to tease her out of a sometimes frosty image, Alex Jones, of *The One Show,* asked Mrs May and her husband about their domestic set-up. Her husband, Philip, revealed that he had to take the bins out but was allowed to decide when – which got a laugh of recognition from the crew.

Theresa, possibly buoyed up by the unfamiliar sound of laughter, chipped in with, 'There are boy jobs and girl jobs, you see.'

Immediately, social media – and Twitter in particular – was ablaze with indignation at this assertion of tired, lazy, sexist, patriarchal (probably fascist) propaganda.

In the skewed cultural world of mainstream media, this became the phone-in subject of choice for the next forty-eight hours: the controversial idea that, in general, men and women living together will often divide tasks along gender lines.

A couple of days later, I was writing on a topical TV show and the production crew continued the outrage at this fusty, out-dated image of the male–female dynamic that this TORY was pushing.

I kept my counsel for a while, then ventured, 'She's right though, isn't she?'

Because she was! It may not be a reality we want to acknowledge in the progressive twenty-twenties, but the idea of pink jobs and blue jobs will still resonate with many people.

So let's accept that they commonly exist, pick a few examples and dig a bit deeper.

TAKING THE BINS OUT = BLUE JOB

There are a number of reasons why blokes might be expected to do this.

Firstly, bins can be heavy, especially if your wife had friends over and the recycling is brimming with empty bottles of Whispering Angel. Bins are on wheels these days but it can take a bit of a heave-ho to shift them. Getting a wheelie bin moving can look as laboured as Granddad getting out of a chair. Almost every woman I know possesses more than enough upper-body strength to move most wheelie bins, but it would take them more effort.

Secondly, the decision to put the bins out is normally something remembered late at night when it's already dark and cold. At this point, the command for the bloke to do it isn't born of natural selection, the woman may just not *want* to venture outside at this time. She's statistically more likely to already be in some form of nightwear (I haven't researched this I just *know*, OK? I'm forty-six and don't know a single bloke who's ever left the house and got in the car still wearing slippers). She'll also still be doing a disproportionate amount of the domestic work and may feel that this late-night task is the very least the bloke can do.

The same theory applies to the evening run to the petrol

station. Sometimes, while watching *Masterchef* or *Bake Off*, you may be so inspired by the complex and artful desserts that you take the cultured decision to go out and buy a Double Decker. In this instance, that mission is almost exclusively a male one (rising to 100 per cent in the event of pregnancy).

WRAPPING PRESENTS = PINK JOB

Full disclosure: like many blokes, I find wrapping anything stressful and would happily let my wife do all of it forever. I also know that however hard I try she's going to look at my finished product askance.

Even when my wrapping is shaping up to be a disaster, I refuse to start again. Where a lot of women will correctly identify it's gone a bit curly and give it another go, I'd rather use three different of types of wrapping paper to get to the job done rather than simply admitting defeat.

The bloke's priority for wrapping is singular: can you see what's underneath the paper? If the answer is 'no', job done. Even if what's covering the present contains elements of tinfoil.

GETTING RID OF SPIDERS = BLUE JOB

Despite women kicking arse all over the employment landscape it remains the case that for many the sight of a spider can have them squealing and standing on a chair like it's the 1950s. In this instance, it's advisable for the bloke to pull the hero move, not least because it involves no bravery whatsoever, given that there aren't any British spiders which are remotely poisonous.

It's probably better for the spiders that it falls to blokes too, as I've seen otherwise gentle women turn to brutal killers the moment anything with eight legs scuttles across a rug.

LOW LEVEL MEDICAL EMERGENCIES IN THE HOUSE = PINK JOB

If there's a cut or bruise in the house, it does seem to fall to women to attend to it. I don't know why this is. Maybe it's all those action films where the hero gets a cut and is dutifully attended to by his female sidekick, who has mysteriously mastered the art of the butterfly stitch. Plus, it also gives him a chance to flinch just a little at the antiseptic, even though he just walked away from an exploding building without flinching.

Or maybe the nursing obligation is all Florence Nightingale's fault.

All I know is that when there are kids involved, and if you ask them, they'd pretty much always prefer a woman to handle such things. They've seen how the blokes in the family approach wrapping presents and packing clothes. They're not idiots.

OK, we've dealt with a couple of age-old classics, but the jobs we do change over time so let's consider where some of the newer household tasks fit into the pink and blue scheme of things.

STAYING ON THE LINE TO A CALL CENTRE FOR A LONG TIME = BLUE JOB

This is clearly one for the blokes.

Although women might spend more time talking on the phone, the gritty business of dispute wrangling is quite clearly the fella's work, as he is often the one blessed with an overdeveloped ego and a pioneering protective bravado. Nothing makes the neutered modern bloke feel quite as powerful as asking to speak to someone's line manager. It's the modern equivalent of pistols at dawn.

Consequently, my yearly job of getting the car insurance company to lower their standard increase back down to a slightly smaller premium is something I undertake with great relish. The guy on the other end better know who he's dealing with. That's right, I'm the legendary fella who was once upgraded by not just one but *two* iPhone models.

PUTTING WINE BOTTLES INTO THE BLUE RECYCLING BIN = BLUE JOB

Look, your neighbours know that you're a lager man but, nevertheless, there's a degree of public shame to depositing drained bottles of Gerard Cordier in recycling – so any true gentleman should happily take that clanking noisy hit. Plus there's an inherent unfairness to redress – a beer drinker could unload a whole weekend's drinking without alerting anyone to their decadence, since empty lager cans barely make a sound (another reason why lager is the best drink).

RETURNING AN UNWANTED ONLINE PURCHASE = PINK JOB

In recent years, I've made a lot of progress with birthday cards (see page 247 for more), but I'm afraid that if I've bought something online and need to return it, I hold it out to my wife pathetically, like a three-year-old boy brandishing his poopy pants.

She's generally more 'match fit' with such things, given that she orders and returns more stuff, but I also don't get how the process works. Not only is it confusing, but returning online purchases often includes the use of stickers and labels, which I deem to be technically arts and crafts and therefore outside my jurisdiction.

Basically, if it was left to me every single out-sized pair of jeans and every electrical item with European plugs would go straight in the bin.

SPORTING HOLY TRINITY #1: FOOTBALL

Supporting the football team your dad followed is the top reason people pick a side.

During the 1980s and 1990s, I followed Wimbledon football club up and down the country. Getting into football isn't unusual; what was peculiar is that it happened despite my family having no tradition of supporting a team whatsoever. In working-class circles this was odd, like a posh family who has no strong feelings about skiing.

There were reasons. My mum had been brought up in care, so there was no partisan legacy on her side. Back then, however, investment in the game would've typically come from your dad anyway. Football allegiance was just one of those things you tended to get from your old man, like eye colour or impatience. But my dad didn't have any pastimes, full stop. If he'd ever been asked to list his hobbies, I suspect they'd have been 'punctuality and mortgages'.

My nan and granddad weren't into football either. Despite living on a council estate, they were into ballroom dancing, which was odd at the time, but you could draw a wonky line from that to the fact that I met my wife on the dancefloor at a nightclub.

Not only were my family not into football, when I started to show an interest in the game they were a bit unnerved. It was the late eighties and the game was blighted by hooliganism. The climate then was very different to now, when stadiums routinely have their share of young goons who've watched *Football Factory*, wear their budget *Peaky Blinders* fancy dress, and spend ninety minutes with their mouth writing cheques their fists could never cash. Back then, naughty things were happening on and off the terraces. My nan, in her oddly prim and regal manner, responded to my emergent love of football in the same way I might react to my son today if he got into bareknuckle boxing.

By the age of nine, I hadn't shown much interest in sport at all, let alone football. But when we moved to a council estate, I quickly realised that I was in a much more blokey environment and needed to fit in. All the men supported teams, as did their sons, who kicked battered footballs around the estate virtually nonstop. I decided I needed to 'man up' and get with the programme. It was one thing having an oddly extended vocabulary for a boy my age, but if I didn't support a football team I could kiss any chance of making friends on the estate goodbye.

I lived every single one of my first fourteen years within spitting distance of Wimbledon FC's original stadium on Plough Lane. In a way, the Dons were a good choice for an already eccentric kid. We weren't one of the best supported teams and didn't have some of the 'nutters' other nearby clubs like Chelsea and Millwall seemed to attract. The ground itself was charmingly ramshackle. Don't get me wrong, matchday was still a manly experience, but my club had plenty of oddball supporters who brought soup in a flask and knitted their own memorabilia. Anyone who followed Wimbledon at that time would tell you that our real thugs were on the pitch, as the squad back then boasted notoriously 'uncompromising' players like Vinnie Jones and John Fashanu. We weren't the most intimidating fans, so we effectively outsourced the aggro to the playing staff. There was a curious tension between how mild our fans could be and how much pleasure we took in yet another opposition player going off on a stretcher.

Even though our fans weren't the most macho, the matchday experience was still replete with some key features of blokeyness: beer, fried food, Bovril, shouting, men standing in each other's company but not together and songs – so many songs.

One of the least understood paradoxes of football is that what's called 'toxic masculinity' sits alongside a patent desire to have a good old sing-song. Yes, some of the chants are akin to battle cries, but others are pretty gentle. Man City sing enigmatic classic 'Blue Moon'. Liverpool belt out the emotionally epic 'You'll Never Walk Alone'. In probably the most unusual case, West Ham sing 'I'm Forever Blowing Bubbles'. There's nothing quite so incongruous as tens of thousands of cockneys singing the line 'and like my dreams they fade and die' – like Doris Day dressed from head to toe in Stone Island.

The templates for terrace chants come from surprisingly un-macho sources: opera, Abba, the Pet Shops Boys. One of the most enduring and recognisable football song structures comes from the disco classic 'Go West'. For all its machismo, football also allows the blokeyest of men to sing their little hearts out like they're doing acapella at a glee club.

I got the football bug pretty bad, aided and abetted by the Wimbledon team of the late eighties punching significantly above their weight. Having only come out of non-league in 1978, we won the FA Cup against the mighty Liverpool in 1988. It was billed as one of the great giant killings of all time, not least because Liverpool had already won the league that year, but it's generally forgotten that we'd finished a not too shabby seventh place. Not only that, we'd beaten Liverpool the season before. So it was David versus Goliath, but if David was only one weight division down and had a horseshoe concealed in his boxing gloves.

Blokes can draw a sense of their character from the team they support. Being a Wimbledon fan was a good moral lesson for me. Their ability to upset the odds gave me the sense that anything was possible, especially with hard work (and a few psychos who could fracture tibias with a look).

Seeing Wembley stadium as a thirteen-year-old was an unforgettable spectacle. So much of what hooks the football fan is those sensory elements. The aesthetic beauty of stadiums themselves, the sight of that many people packed into one place, the smells of the food, the sounds of the chanting. I'd often get into the ground long before kick-off just to sit amid the experience for as long as I could.

A lot of football fans have an early taste of euphoria, which gets them hooked. My moment came watching that famous Wimbledon team upset the odds to win the cup, like a gambler whose first bet was a rank 20/1 outsider which romped home.

However, as with all gambling, unless you support the biggest clubs, the losses can eventually mount up. At 5pm on a Saturday, there will be hundreds of thousands of blokes who didn't get what they want and enter into a giant man-sulk about events beyond their control. It must seem odd that this creature who panics when asked what he's thinking and rarely expresses emotions is suddenly having a hissy fit in front of Sky Sports waving his arms around like an Italian chef. Football serves as an emotional conduit for men all around the world, but given the reputation the British have for being reserved, it's no surprise that a lot of our latent emotions come out within the confines of football stadiums and that the intense atmosphere of our domestic games is one of the reasons it's such a successful export. (Who'd have thought our dads not hugging us would ultimately help sell Premier League rights in Malaysia?)

All of which is partly why a bloke will regularly and ruminatively comment that 'the game's changed'. I suspect blokes have been claiming the 'game's changed' ever since its inception. When goalkeepers started wearing gloves. When players stopped emerging for the second half finishing a cigarette; and when you could no longer punch the opposition's best player into the foetal position. These days, my pals constantly talk about how they don't 'feel' it like they used to. Some of that is down to the way the game has undergone radical commercial change over the last twenty years, but it's also a consequence of advancing years. Middle-aged men take a while to work out that their relationship with the joy of football has fundamentally changed, like teenagers confused as to why they no longer rush downstairs on Christmas morning. Some try to keep the intensity by drinking loads or betting large sums of money, but the true wonder of football will always be felt most keenly by the young.

One tangible effect of the increasing foreign ownership of Premiership teams has been to add a further layer between the current function of the game and its original purpose. The words 'football club' have a genuine meaning. People often don't stop to think about the 'club' bit. It's a place to go, to be around friends, people to talk to, something else to focus on at the end of another hard week.

In the Birmingham area, Aston Villa and Birmingham City arose in part out of a desire to create places where the scores of antisocial young men who'd been causing mischief could go on a Saturday afternoon, to keep them out of gangs like the Peaky Blinders. In a football stadium they might still act up but at least it was contained (though far less likely to form the basis for a successful BBC drama).

In the same way that boxing clubs were a way of channelling aggression, going to the football can be like a version of primal scream therapy, where the process of venting feelings doesn't result in you feeling like a muppet. Not only that, you can take the piss out of cosseted millionaires who've owned a Bentley since they were fifteen. It's a bargain, really.

If you think that for a bloke, football is about football, you're missing the point. It's called 'the beautiful game' but as an aesthetic experience the sport doesn't really compare to the pristine look of cricket or the kinetic joy of tennis. The intensity of the game is derived from the scarcity of scoring opportunities. That's how those big emotions get released. In every fan there is a balloon waiting to pop. They're not ecstatic because they watched eighty-nine minutes of drudgery. It's that one minute, that one moment where they could truly let go, scream at the top of their lungs and hug a stranger. Consequently, men who didn't cry at their own parent's funeral can safely transfer that emotion to going out of the Carabao Cup on penalties.

When West Ham left their spiritual home of Upton Park, there were numerous videos of tough-looking working-class men crying their eyes out at the closure of their historic ground. They were mocked for shows of incongruous sentimentality, but people seemed to not get it: football is one grand analogy, and like all analogies it only works when you're throwing other, seemingly unconnected things into the mix. Those same people mocking the West Ham fans might well have been distraught when Paris's Notre-Dame cathedral burned down in 2019. You could throw the same argument back at them: 'It's just a building'. But of course Notre-Dame wasn't 'just' a building and neither was Upton Park just a stadium. It was a place where fans purged a bunch of feelings they couldn't find an outlet for elsewhere.

If those men found they couldn't let those feelings go in their real lives, then so much the better that they could do it somewhere.

CHAINED TO A MADMAN: A BLOKE'S SEXUAL LIFE

*The average age at which British men lose
their virginity is 18.3 years old.*

Despite all the advances in gender equality, blokes still feel it's their job to take the lead on initiating things in the romance department. Asking women out on dates, going in for the first kiss, suggesting sex . . . then pretending you were only joking when all those suggestions crash and burn horribly.

You might dismiss the burden of initiation as being 'just how it is', but I refer you to a 2016 poll which revealed that men might not be so happy with the status quo. The poll explored the top five grievances the two sexes have with each other. Women's top five focused more on domestic issues, like him leaving the toilet seat up, not tidying after himself . . . continuing to draw breath. One of British men's top grievances, however, was that it always fell to them to initiate sex. I can hear some women groaning and playing tiny imaginary violins, but as men hit middle age the process of kickstarting romance becomes a harder mountain to climb (not least when you're dealing with only three solid erections per month).

It's a very different story in their youth, when blokes have a full tank of testosterone and several natural drivers which make the risk of initiating sexual activity seem like a reasonable gamble with their self-esteem. In some ways, you don't have a choice – that madman between your legs often puts your mind on autopilot (this is not to excuse men for the worst behaviours around sex – like all autopilots, the real pilot should be on hand, sober enough to make the correct calls if you hit turbulence). In your formative sexual years, the urge to have sex is an impulse created on your behalf, something your body and subconscious decided on long before you took that nervous walk towards a nice-looking woman in a pub. Like the salmon swimming back upstream, you continue walking in her direction even if it looks like she just rolled her eyes.

Seduction in general has long been a particular problem for the British bloke. Try to think of a particularly British way a man could 'seduce' a woman. What comes to mind?

The most obvious archetype is the bumbling posh bloke. Hugh Grant dithering over his words and slowly winning the woman over. This is bollocks. The only person the Hugh Grant approach works for is Hugh Grant, who has the ultimate advantage of actually being Hugh Grant. In my experience, dragging out the process of asking a woman on a date or for a kiss is rarely endearing. It makes you look indecisive and weak. I don't want to sound too Andrew Tate, but I think it's fair to say that there's no amount of gender equality which would render acting like a sap sexually attractive.

For men, rolling the dice always involves a combination of faith and – above all – energy: the sheer will to keep returning to the pontoon table of sex.

By adulthood, the average male will have experienced far more sexual rejections in his life than a woman. 'Crashing and burning' is an unavoidable rite of passage for any bloke. It's the most crushing feeling imaginable, but also the thing most likely to make your mates piss themselves laughing. The joy in the eyes of your friends when you get 'pied off' by a girl is hard to quantify. We've all known it. The only time you'll ever see your best mate happier is if you got smashed in the nuts by a cricket ball. If a man ever asks me what it's like to have a terrible comedy gig I tell him it's like getting brushed off by a girl in front of 400 people. You can see it in his eyes, he knows what I mean. He's glimpsed that void.

During your thirties, the male libido can be given an additional lease of life by the fact that the woman you're with has decided she doesn't after all want to devote her life to listening to your music recommendations and generally having a laugh, she now wants to have a kid.

Many men moan about the expectation to perform during attempts to conceive but you have to view it positively: is it 'pressure'? Or 'guaranteed shagging'? It's ironic that the bloke complaining about becoming a 'sexual object on demand' is now the exact emotional creature his partner once yearned for and at just the point she needs him to deliver the goods and stop whining like a little bitch.

By your mid-forties, however, once baby-making is largely concluded, sex is something very different: it's become an activity couples are vaguely conscious they should engage in every so often – a cross between a leisure pursuit and something on a to-do list, like getting the dog groomed or visiting relatives. Whenever you *do* get down to it, the two of you seem to have a pleasant enough time, but part of that euphoria comes from having temporarily ticked something off the list. And if you conclude the act with enough time to watch an episode of *Below Deck*, happy days. It can feel less like a hot act of steamy lovemaking and more like you've just done the big shop.

Once you've hit a certain age, it's also all the better for coming as a pleasant surprise. It's like walking home from the pub and thinking, 'Blimey, I was *not* expecting to see Halley's Comet tonight. Bonus.'

While most blokes will recognise libido as a tide which eventually has to recede – not entirely unwelcome, given all the energy it's consumed and humiliation it has caused – a declining sexual drive can lead men to do crazy things. Some blokes aren't willing to disappear into their sexual twilight without a fight. They look for ways of feeling like that mad horny teenager once more, which leads them to make all manner of Faustian pacts.

Some middle-aged men forget the happiness and additional life expectancy which a stable marriage affords and go off with a younger woman. I don't doubt that it would be exciting to have a younger lover. I'm sure your penis – that madman in charge of the Light Brigade who has led you to so many glorious defeats – would be delighted. But the question all men must ask themselves on the point of such a decision is this: 'Will the sex be so good it compensates for the trauma of a divorce?' And: 'Does my penis have a great track record when it comes to making big life decisions? Especially bearing in mind how many random erections I got during that GCSE maths exam.'

So a true British bloke will eventually arrive at a very different relationship with sex. If he does seem a lot less interested in having it these days, just bear in mind that he's the veteran of many bruising campaigns. He's crashed and burned many times. He is both Goose and Maverick . . . but mostly Goose.

And – just like a lady wearing her Bridget Jones big knickers – him wearing socks *and* sandals in the front room around bedtime may be his unique way of asking you to accept that, on this occasion, no means no.

TALL PRIVILEGE

*Five foot nine is the average height for a
UK male . . . I swear to God it is!*

The advent of dating apps formalised something in the male/
female dynamic which we'd lost sight of over time: for most
women, it's important for blokes to be tall – or at the very least,
taller than them.

If you look at women's dating profiles, many are prescriptive
about the kind of height they're looking for in a fella. Some say
'no short men', some will even set a benchmark figure, such as
six foot, like the dating equivalent of height restrictions at theme
parks (except more crushing because those rules may eventually
mean you die alone).

How many times have you heard a woman not only stipulate
that their bloke has to be taller than them, but go on to place the
further hurdle: 'He's got to be taller than me when I'm wearing
heels.' Just to make things even harder, they've artificially added
anything from two to six inches to their height and declared this
to be the new benchmark. Yet if a bloke turns up to a date
wearing platform shoes apparently he's the weirdo.

When it comes to specificity about physical attributes, we're
living in a very different time, where women are able to be
fairly direct about what they're looking for while men have had
to become ever more euphemistic when it comes to their
aesthetic preferences. A bloke would rightly expect to get very

few matches if he wrote in his bio, 'Nothing lower than a C cup'.

It's odd that the preference for men to be taller has been so persistent over time. It comes from a woman's ancient and reasonable impulse to find an effective protector. If she were significantly taller than him and there was a bear on the loose, the woman could find the guy shrugging apologetically and holding the door open for her, nodding suggestively towards the perils of the outside world.

If we're honest, on a purely aesthetic level it does look incredibly weird when you see a woman who is significantly taller than her man. It's one of life's odder images, like seeing a cat on a lead. However, in an odd way, a big height difference seems to work better than a small one: if you're going to go shorter, go a LOT shorter. Seeing a tall woman pull a very short man to her plentiful bosom is never not funny.

For blokes who haven't owned Playboy mansions or appeared in buddy comedies with Arnold Schwarzenegger, height is another crucial attribute we can do nothing about. That stark reality is made all the harder once you know the benefits that tall males enjoy.

A study published by the American National Bureau of Economic Research suggested that taller men report greater levels of contentment, and are less likely to experience sadness or, somewhat astonishingly, physical pain.

Physical pain? What the actual fuck? This isn't just a fringe benefit; their lives are better on a cellular level. It's like finding out that men with large penises have more enjoyable orgasms. (Do they? Actually, I'd rather not know.)

Tall men also statistically earn more and are more likely to impress at job interviews. They're also more likely to be respected by their male peers. The list of benefits is huge. Or 'tall'.

Until fairly recently, I had, for some reason, harboured the idea I was five foot ten. I used to mention this belief on stage and people would frown, shake their heads and sometimes openly laugh at me. In the fullness of time they were proved right – I'm five foot eight and a quarter. But the fact that I couldn't even conjure up enough inner confidence to project the idea I might be a mere inch and a half taller was disappointing.

Whatever the average male height is, the standard idea of a 'good height' for a man in Britain is six foot. This means a lot of men around my height still get called 'short' when we statistically are not (am I sounding enough like a chippy short guy yet?). In fact, if you aggregate all the male heights globally, British men of average stature would still be taller than a significant majority of everyone alive today.

I sometimes surprise my wife with this knowledge when we're on a tube train. The low ceiling of the London Underground makes relative height easier to discern. In a busy carriage, I can point out to her just how many of the thirty or so people within sight I'm taller than. It's not much of a boast, more the law of averages: once you take into account women, children and the half of all men I'm taller than, that puts me mathematically well into the top 25 per cent.

And yet audiences continue to laugh when I claim that I'm not short, like some vertically challenged Pinocchio insisting 'I'm a real boy!'

So, anyway . . . It would seem that rather than being short, not being tall is the greater Achilles heel, the worse crime. Napoleon is a prime example. Widely considered to epitomise little man syndrome, he was actually five foot five (or so he said). That was the average height for a Frenchman at the time, yet it still wasn't enough and he's considered one of history's great short arses (I moan a bit, but at least I never took revenge by invading half of Europe).

The mockery of men of below average height can be brutal. In the original *Shrek*, the running joke about Lord Farquaad is simply that he's very short. At one point, Shrek and Donkey do an extended pun-off on the subject.

How must it feel to be a genuinely short young boy watching that film for the first time? At the same time as his sister is watching animated films with brave female leads and adverts promoting body positivity, everyone is falling about laughing over a male character's genetics.

Our current prime minister (let's be honest, there might have been three more by the time this gets published) Rishi Sunak is a diminutive five foot six. He's faced a lot of open mockery for this. *The Huffington Post* ran a piece on the subject in which they sensitively republished a lot of the most hurtful insults, just to, y'know, show you how seriously they were taking male height-shaming. Though they did go on to say that it was wrong and hurtful, about two thirds of the way down, after a clutch of mocking tweets and by the time most readers had lost the will to live.

Rishi is clearly conscious of how his height affects people's perception of him. A lot of his photos have people standing distances apart not seen since the height of Covid. And who can blame him when you consider the value society puts on tall men? Tom Cruise is only too aware: it's the reason he's been practically walking on stilts since the early eighties.

Analysis has shown that, on dating sites, men who stood at around six foot three got 60 per cent more messages than blokes around five foot seven and eight.

Sixty per cent!

It's like a version of the dating show *Take Me Out* where any man under six foot who comes down that elevator not only gets buzzed off but gets fired straight into space.

So much stock is put on height, but basic differences in stature are often less stark than the optics suggest. If you compare a successful, extremely tall celebrity like Richard Osman against a much-loved shorty like Sandi Toksvig, you'd be forgiven for thinking that he's twice her height. He's not. Richard is a grand 200cm, but Sandi is 152cm. Which means, somewhat unbelievably, that he's only 24 per cent taller.

This is reassuring for a guy like me. Think of a handsome basketball player who's six foot nine. Believe it or not, he's only 14 per cent taller than me (though, for a lot of reasons, his dating site DMs would probably be much more than 14 per cent busier than mine).

Height is another thing, like penis size, which matters to a lot of women but which men can't do anything about. The superficial features of female beauty – hair, eyes, eyelashes, lips, cheeks, boobs – can all be enhanced in different ways. Blokes literally cannot make themselves taller (well, they can, but it involves some bizarre operation where they break both your legs, so your family don't know if you had self-esteem issues or defaulted on a debt to a loan shark).

Interestingly, the National Bureau of Economic Research study also found that men most likely to call their lives the 'worst possible' were an inch shorter than average. This makes sense.

It's better to die having never known of the promised land than have glimpsed it up close. This might be why I'm so exercised on the subject . . . perhaps I should reveal my hand, as there's a chance I have too much skin in this game.

At the age of twelve, I was already my current height and my doctor reckoned I would hit 'at least' six foot. There's a photo of me at the end of Year 7 standing head and shoulders above all my classmates. I got used to the comments tall guys get: 'Did you fall asleep in a greenhouse?', 'They been feeding you raw meat?', 'Have you been held back a year?'

The problem was that I suddenly stopped growing. Not just for the next year or so, but for the rest of my life. The height I'd reached at twelve was as tall as I'd ever be. This was a cruel way for my final adult height to unfold. One September, I went back to school and lads I'd lorded it over six weeks previously were now patting me on the head. I still hate getting a hug from taller men. Not only does it make me feel like less of a man; I also feel like a sibling going around the giant house of a brother who inherited everything.

So if you ever see me on stage or in print trying desperately to be taken seriously as a man of five foot nine, please bear mind that I was once destined for more – so much more.

GEOFFREY THE GIRAFFE

Question. Are you a woman reading this? If yes, are you married to a working-class bloke? If the answer to that is also 'yes' now turn to him and ask him if any of his friends have funny nicknames.

Enjoy the next two hours.

You're welcome.

Nicknames aren't the sole preserve of working-class men, but it does seem to be a cultural phenomenon where we over-represent. I'm not saying middle-class blokes spend their lives calling each other solely by Christian names, but what they call nicknames often amount to adding a 'y' at the end of a surname.

I can't recall exactly when me and my mates started dabbling with nicknames. Small children had them at school, but they tended to be route one and cruel. If you pissed your pants in assembly you probably got called 'pissy pants' (personally, I'd add a 'captain' at the beginning for creativity, but that's just me).

When I was at primary school, there was a popular book called *Geoffrey the Giraffe*. The moment I saw my teacher holding that title, I knew I was in trouble. My classmates all started singing 'Geoffrey the Giraffe' in that sarcastic, teasing way small kids have a habit of doing. I didn't even know why I was so upset, there are worse animals to be compared to than a giraffe, but as is often the case, alliteration had a persuasive power way beyond its actual function (and the irony of that taunt would be even more hurtful today given what I've already revealed about my height).

As we became teenagers, the nicknames grew a little more complex and ironic.

One day, I asked my mate Mick if he'd come with me to a football trial. He asked who was organising it and I said it was a bloke called 'Lofty'. Mick said he couldn't go because he'd already committed to attending a trial organised by a 'Danny White'. When I got to the training ground I was surprised to see Mick there. Being dumb young men, it took us far too long to work out that 'Lofty' and 'Danny White' were the same person. It was like an extremely low-rent version of the end of *Usual Suspects* when the investigating officer lets his mug fall to the floor.

Danny was our Keyser Söze.

He was also called Lofty because . . . wait for it . . . he wasn't actually tall. It all seems fairly obvious and basic now, but back then we were only just starting to explore irony (and the value of characters from *It Ain't Half Hot Mum*). As the years rolled on we got more creative, to the point where a bloke being called Lofty could just have meant he liked lofts.

One early complex nickname was born when my mate Rick threw his joypad across the room because he couldn't handle being continually beaten at Pete Sampras Tennis on the Sega Mega Drive. We called him 'Fatima', a reference to that famous athlete's supreme javelin lobbing skills and just how far that joypad travelled (it was a big lounge and the thing almost flew out the window).

The problem was that his nickname became so ingrained we stopped saying 'Fatima' with irony, so new friends were left confused when our mate, the mysterious 'Fatima', turned out to be a painfully white lad from Scarborough.

There were other legends of the nickname game. 'Fireplace Jack', so called because he had sex in a fireplace. Then there's my mate we call 'Gary'. He got that name because he looks like another of our mates called Gary, who we now call 'Original Gary'. Imagine how pissed off he is at not even being the foremost Gary in a group of mates where he's the only bloke actually called Gary.

There are plenty of nicknames born of one man showing limited and temporary expertise in a given field. There's 'Magnus', who got his name after the former *University Challenge* host Magnus Magnusson, following a semi decent run on a pub quiz machine. And 'GBJ', which is short for 'Genius Bar Jim' – who simply knew how to reset my brother-in-law's MacBook.

Nicknames can be fun, but they can also run the risk of immortalising things you'd rather forget.

Once, in Berlin, we were running low on alcohol. All we had left was sambuca, so we poured (rationed) all the remaining measures into a selection of shot glasses. There was a well-marshalled process for calling each man up for his latest dose, but things inevitably got drunken and distracted. As the man in charge of this process, however, I was hypervigilant. I got a sense from Danny's body language that, amid the drunk fog of war, he was up to no good. As he stepped up to the table in the corner of the room, he had a quick look over one shoulder, then slammed an illegal second shot. I very quickly said, 'Check out old Danny two shots!'

Danny's face fell, not least because he knew he'd been caught, but also because he realised that the nickname scanned well enough for it to have a good chance of sticking. On the plus side, it sounded pretty cool – 'Danny two shots' brought to mind one of Joe Pesci's mates in *Goodfellas*. The problem was that nothing gives blokes more pleasure than unpacking a nickname, so ever since that day, Danny has had to take repeated punishment beatings as we relay his origins story.

One of my favourite nicknames is 'Dead Steve'. Steve's moniker was a complicated one. He got it back in the early nineties when he went to Thailand for a month. Back then, we didn't know anyone who went away that far and for that long. Without mobile phones or even email, we had no idea as to Steve's welfare. As two weeks became three then three turned into four, rumours started to circulate. Once a whole month had gone by, we could only conclude that Steve was in fact dead. The rumour went around south London like wildfire.

'You heard about dead Steve?'

'What's happened?'

'There's a clue in the name.'

Luckily, Steve is still with us, but none of us is getting any younger and at some point it might make sense to give him a quick rebrand.

One thing you can never do is pick your own nickname. Over the years, I've known some who've tried. Back in the early noughties I thought (hoped) that I looked a bit like Joey from *Friends* and considered that this could be a useful comparison from the point of view of attracting ladies (and excusing my habits around food). I tried to casually insinuate that a few people had started calling me 'Joey', or whatever, and shrugged with the forced oversell of the patent liar.

The lads rounded on me pretty quickly and gave my attempted nickname a tweak. I didn't mind really. So long as they called me something. One of the great things about becoming friends with other blokes is that you feel like you've been born again into a slightly different family. The one thing any family wants to do with a new arrival is to give it its own name.

It's just a shame that, having hoped to be named after one of the sexiest men on telly, I quickly got christened 'Fat le Blanc'.

HEROES OF BLOKEDOM #2: ADRIAN CHILES

My second blokey hero is also someone I've had the privilege of working with: Adrian Chiles.

In a way, saying Adrian Chiles is my hero is a very Adrian Chiles thing to do.

In the past few years, as well as being a terrific broadcaster, he's carved out a niche writing for the *Guardian*, producing articles which are not only outside the publication's usual social and political bias, but are also unique in their celebration of mundane and noble preoccupations, something the average bloke tends towards.

Here are a few of Adrian's best titles to savour:

'If dishwashers were a sport, my dad would be world champion.'

'All you can eat? I take those words as a promise and a challenge.'

'An ear and nostril waxing is exquisitely painful – but just what I needed.'

There are so many. Chiles once extolled the virtues of having a urinal in his home toilet and, while the world was obsessing over war and pestilence, he went off on one about why he hates sand.

There are some in metropolitan circles who enjoy his low-level ranting in the same way they enjoy professional darts – ironically.

I don't. I just think he's shrewd enough to know that his everyday brand of blokery strikes a genuine chord with millions of people. It's not an 'angle'; it's a faithful reflection of the small things which can feel so big in daily life.

For a time, newspapers, populated as they largely are by urban middle-class professionals, wrongly concluded that all we want to read about is Brexit, or whether misgendering should come with a custodial sentence. Chiles knows differently. Life is already stressful, so it's preferrable to get exercised about the little things – not least because those are problems we at least stand some chance of resolving. His articles succeed for the same reason programmes about bargains and gardens succeed: in the real world, that's what people truly care about. Ask anyone who hates sand about sand. They'll get way more exercised about that than whether sports pundits should tweet about refugees. Chiles comes across as the kind of bloke who could solve most of the world's problems with a pint and a squirt of WD-40.

I'm not sure whether the act of falling into conversation with some random geezer at a pub is a thing any more. Was it ever? The kind of men who speak to strangers in pubs are usually rampant alcoholics only ever a moment away from saying something genuinely dodgy. Chiles, however, really does seem to be the bloke you might get into a good chat with: informed yet informal, giving off the reassuring vibe of a man who always has the correct Allen key to hand.

I remember the first time I saw Chiles on telly. It was in the mid-nineties and he was co-presenting a show called *Working Lunch*. Even the name 'Adrian Chiles' carried with it an air of Midlands chumminess. Post diversity targets, we're more used to hearing working-class accents on the Beeb – but back then, his broad Brummie tones stood out in a bland sea of Received Pronunciation, particularly in the world of 'serious' broadcasting. You have to remember that this was before the Midlands twang underwent a trendy rehabilitation at the hands of the Peaky Blinders. Back then, when we thought of the Midlands we were thinking of Noddy Holder rather than Tommy Shelby.

Adrian seemed confident and informed while also coming across like one of your dad's most likeable mates. The accent helped in establishing him as normal. With all respect, it's very hard to imagine anyone from this part of the country as part of the liberal elite. I had no idea what his upbringing was like but filed him away as working class. Even today, he could be sipping kombucha on the slopes at Davos and still sound like he bulk-buys from Aldi.

His common-touch expertise echoed the world I lived in at the time. My dad's mates down the pub were all fairly political and clued up. Having been adult men during the volatile 1970s, they discussed public affairs all the time, but when it came to politics on the telly or radio the glottal well and truly stopped.

One of Chiles's other great strengths is that I've never had an idea of how he might vote. It's not cool in blokey circles to get preachy. He has a knack of getting irritated rather than angry, which helps make him seem authentic to the watching public. It's refreshing at a time when, via a string of big stories like Brexit and Covid, journalism became a seriously high-status profession.

When Dominic Cummings sat in the rose garden at Number Ten behind that trestle table, like he was about to serve homemade lemonade at a country fete, the journos queued up to grill him about driving to Durham, but mostly delivered what sounded like GCSE drama monologues. The situation was crying out for someone like Chiles to chime in like an everyman and say, 'Hang on just a minute, you drove to check your *eyesight*??'

Chiles, through not over-speaking or emoting, seems both authentic and authoritative. There are no long words simply for their own sake. No showboating. Even when he wrote an excellent book on drinking habits, he didn't do the showbiz thing of lurching from over-indulgence to abstinence, he simply put forward an argument for drinking less.

This is how most people think, and though his life today may well be rarefied and fairly wealthy, Adrian Chiles, with his ability to seem exceptional in his unexceptionalism, will always feel like the quintessential British Bloke.

FANCY A CURRY?

Just like being asked if you fancy a pint, 'Wanna go for a ruby?' is up there with the best questions you could ask any bloke (not least because a curry also tends to involve several lagers).

Going for a curry skews blokey. I've seen plenty of women in curry houses over the years, but it's rare that I've witnessed a raucous group of ladies enter the Raj Douth after a day on the ale and order thirty-two poppadoms and eight Cobras before they've even sat down.

So what's the connection between blokes and going for a curry?

The first big draw is that a curry is perceived as an informal way to dine. It's often a spontaneous adjunct to a whole day spent together, usually drinking. You hit that point where things will either get really messy or you recognise food intake to be crucial (either that or several of your mates' knees are playing up and you need somewhere you can be guaranteed a seat). I'm not saying I haven't booked restaurants for a group of blokes before, but it's been rare, and canvassing opinion for food options too early on a lads' WhatsApp group can result in a whole day of ridicule (and yet another new nickname). This differs as you move through the class brackets, though. Among more middle-class blokes, it's not unheard of for people to mention TripAdvisor ratings and query who the chef trained with.

The standard curry-house experience, however, is a different beast. A lot of their trade is made up of large groups of blokes making a sudden decision to add further digestive problems to the following day. As an establishment, a curry house knows how to cope with a huge influx of men and they rarely mess about asking if you've booked (you've never booked). There's also a lack of protocols at a curry house. If I went to a fancy place with my wife she might shoot me a look if I started asking for table bread too early, but the fact you'll have poppadoms is generally a given and will be confirmed as the waiter takes your coat.

The poppadoms themselves epitomise the informal nature of the curry-house experience. Bread rolls need to be daintily buttered but poppadoms get smashed to pieces within minutes.

As blokes often communicate in analogies, how you eat a poppadom can be a good way of telling the group who you are. Any man who brings his fist down on the whole pile without first consulting the group has established himself as a wannabe alpha. Blokes who just pick up a shard of poppadom and randomly scoop it in the pots and sauces are rank-and-file heathens, but a clearly thought-out and structured approach represents peak blokery. I tend to find a decent-sized piece, normally approximately an eighth the size of the entire poppadom, and think of it more of a pizza on which to put toppings. I don't want to have so many onions that I need to spend the following day adopting Covid levels of social distancing, and nor do I want so much mango chutney that it feels like I've already started my dessert. By showing such forethought I could be easily construed as fancy or fussy, but it's neither – I just love having a curry and am confident enough in my own process not to be swept along with the herd.

When it comes to poppadoms, the only thing up for debate is the number, plus an unequivocal promise that they'll bring out the lime pickle.

Lime pickle used to be a standard feature of the poppadom condiments but somewhere in the late noughties it became a treat you had to ask for, like the curry equivalent of under-the-counter medication. This move may have been an act of charity by the restaurant itself. When you overdo a curry, a lot of the acid comes from the pickle, containing as it does a devastating combination of chilli and lime. If they really wanted to show customer care they wouldn't bring out After Eights at the end of the meal, it would be a tray of Rennies.

However, the jeopardy of spice levels opens up another element of curry's appeal to the blokey mentality: it engages with the attraction to risk.

There's something of the Vegas casino about going for a curry. You could get the balance right and have a great meal with no enduring legacy. Or you could overreach, leave with the hiccups and be up at 5am the following morning with your backside on fire, seeing if Just Eats delivers omeprazole. In the same way that car parks absolve themselves of responsibility for any thefts which happen within them, it would make sense for a curry house to remind patrons that 'All choices made within this establishment are your own. If you're pushing fifty and order anything stronger than a dopiaza, you've only got yourself to blame.'

A curry house is one of few places where the drinks order is posed more in the form of a rhetorical question. 'Nine Cobras?' That's the starting point for the waiter. If you're going to showboat and order something different it's on you to explain yourself. Cobra is such a great recent accompaniment to curry that I shudder to think of the gassier alternatives I used to wash down a jalfrezi with.

It was designed with curry in mind. When Labour leader Keir Starmer faced questions over 'Beergate' allegations in Durham, the political class obsessed over whether or not he'd broken lockdown rules. The police eventually decided he hadn't, but for a lot of the British public we'd come to our own verdict: the man drank San Miguel with a curry and was therefore a psychopath. I'm not saying you can *only* drink Cobra, but it had better be something damn similar.

With the poppadom and lager choices settled, the real opportunity for bravado begins: your choice of main.

I'm not saying a bloke should *never* have a korma, but if he does he should at the very least explain why. I just don't know why you'd go for a meal with such flavour potential as a curry but choose something so childlike as a chicken korma. It's like going to a theme park and making a beeline for the magic teacups. If you're genuinely worried about the level of spice have a bit of tandoori chicken. Even this turns out to be a bit on the flavoursome side: tandoori comes with the cucumber raita for you to dive into, like a culinary plunge-pool just outside the sauna.

Once upon a time, I'd have gone quite high up the heat scale, usually ordering a madras, and sometimes a vindaloo. I had a decent tolerance for hot curries given that, for the first nine years of my life, I had a surrogate Indian family living upstairs who I spent a lot of time with. I used to trot up there regularly and, even as a six-year-old, was dealing OK with the dopiazas and bhunas of this world.

I was, for a time, something of a novelty. When they had Indian relatives over, they would all want to see the phenomenon of this little white boy polishing off spicy dishes for themselves. They'd crowd around, marvelling at me knocking back a masala like I was a character from the director's cut of *The Greatest Showman*. Consequently, curry always meant more to me than just the dish itself – it took me back to a much-loved part of my childhood. But like anyone who gets a buzz from something, you eventually go looking for bigger kicks.

For a long time, vindaloo was the apex predator of my curry world, but some time in the late nineties there were dark murmurings about a dish called a 'phaal'.

I had to try it.

In the curry house, I made a big deal of ordering the phaal, confidently telling the waiters that I was effectively half Indian so it shouldn't pose too much of a problem.

I still remember the moment the heat kicked in. It wasn't on the first or second mouthful but somewhere around the third when my body started going into violent revolution against my foolish choices. I gave the waiter a look which must have been like the accusatory one people throw when they realise they've been poisoned. Then I got the most savage hiccups I'd ever had. The waiters started to look genuinely concerned and I ended up doing shots of cucumber raita like I was in a head-to-head drinking competition with a teetotal vegetarian.

It wasn't the last time my bravado would undo me either.

In 2013, I was doing some gigs for the British armed forces in Cyprus and we had the honour of performing for a Gurkha regiment.

The Gurkhas enjoyed the gig and invited us to dine with them afterwards. I got the sense they might try to test our capacity for Nepalese cuisine and noticed some of the soldiers cautiously watching us after each course.

I thought I'd withstood the best of what they had to offer when the chef finally brought out what looked like a very plain plate of chicken nuggets. I laughed, surprised, and held one up to a lad who'd been watching me intently, making a 'is this the best you have to offer?' gesture. His gaze didn't change, and I'd soon come to realise that it was the unbreakable glare of the stone-cold assassin.

I don't know what was in those chicken nuggets, but I'd eaten about three before I got any sense of how much trouble I was in. It wasn't just a chicken nugget; it was a sleeper cell of fire. There was a devilish delayed release from the spice within. The heat was happening not in my mouth or throat but somewhere deep in the pit of my stomach, like a culinary depth charge.

I was determined not to give away how much I was struggling but, like any man trying to throw out an immovable poker face, sweating was something I wasn't in control of. Thank God I wasn't in a Pizza Express.

With the gaze of the guy who'd taken me out still upon me, I decided to double down. I couldn't let him 'win', so, with sweat streaming down my face and a fire happening in my gizzards, I took a couple more nuggets and ate them. He cheered. The sweats got worse but I kept going and spent the whole of the following day in the bad place.

That day, I proved something to those lads. I can't tell you exactly what, or whether it was worth it, but I got the sense that my willingness to endure pain for honour had won me respect. (Though none of them ate the chicken nuggets, so I might've proved myself a reliable comrade or just been the evening's entertainment.)

This is the power of spicy food and, more specifically, a curry. Nowhere else does the simple selection of your main course offer scope for acts of true daring and heroism. For blokes, it can be not just a meal but a full-on adventure.

'Dear, I always say,
a flawed husband is
better than none at all.'
Mrs Doubtfire

BLOKEY FILM REVISIONS #2: MARY POPPINS

As we know, at heart, the modern bloke is a sentimental softy and while he may publicly say that he only watches films with Tom Hardy or an aeroplane containing Samuel L Jackson and some snakes, secretly he's delighted to be watching *Frozen* again with his kids (although he may have to come up with a creative explanation for why his eyes are streaming when Olaf the Snowman starts to melt).

Accordingly, one of my top five favourite films is surprisingly soppy: *Mary Poppins.*

Don't laugh. In my defence, I should add that the other four are *The Empire Strikes Back*, *Avengers: Endgame*, *Goodfellas* and *Top Gun: Maverick* (imagine me now crushing a plastic cup like Brody in *Jaws*).

I always loved *Mary Poppins*; we used to watch it at least once a year growing up, often around Easter. In her own way, my mum had a touch of the Poppins about her – a funny and, in some ways, mystical woman who always had surprising things in her handbag.

At first, I understood the film as I was supposed to: Jane and Michael were good kids in need of more attention; the wife was a bit distracted but otherwise a nice enough lady and Mr Banks was the well-meaning villain of the piece who needed to loosen up and join in the fun. He was always coming home from work

97

in a grump and ruining everyone's fun. The idea struck a chord at that point in my life, as my own dad could sometimes feel a little separate from the main business of the house. He too had some weird job in London I didn't fully understand. The fact that Banks was British also felt important. There have been plenty of Hollywood films since which have dealt with the issue of busy and emotionally distant dads, but the idea seems particularly resonant when merged with the British stiff upper lip.

However, as I've got older and my own responsibilities have started to mount up, I've started to view old Banks in a very different light.

Why is Mr Banks the villain of this piece at all? He's clearly grafted his whole life in a toxically masculine workplace to finance a lovely gaff slap bang in the middle of London (although presumably the estate agent knocked a few guineas off the asking price because of the daily damage done by the next-door neighbour firing an actual cannon every bloody day of the week). Is it too much to ask that when he gets home of an evening his kids aren't being collared by the local bobby and his Mrs isn't constantly out at feminist rallies like an early prototype of an Islington mother? Votes for Women is a noble cause but Banks can't be expected to be the sole breadwinner *and* stop his kids going off the rails at the same time as his wife is chaining herself to them.

Banks is clearly a decent bloke at heart; he's just slightly out of step with the rest of the family. He tries to join in, doesn't he? He even sings a song, albeit reluctantly, like an older member of staff at a company karaoke, but at least he has a go. And in his song he quite rightly points out that he'd like a bit of discipline in the family, some basic rules to live by. Who can disagree when he says he doesn't want 'disaster and catastrophe' in the house?

Surely that's the first aim of any responsible father, isn't it? Apparently not. Apparently that makes him a stick-in-the-mud who doesn't approve of a strange woman encouraging his kids to dance on a rooftop without a safety harness. And yet, when he merely tries to demonstrate the value of money his kids start acting up like he's taking them for a root canal.

All that poor sod wanted was to get home, kick off his spats, have a nice plate of liver and onions and watch a magic lantern show with the family while they ask him how his day was. And, of course, the answer to that question would be, 'The same as every other bloody day, a waking nightmare of class snobbery and excruciating boredom.' Except he would never articulate that thought because the conscientious bloke wants to protect his family from the crushing truth of reality.

Into this bargain comes Mary Poppins, who I do fully love – and was my first crush – but, let's be honest, she's a vain woman and an absolute loose cannon. She introduces a strange brand of socially acceptable voodoo into the Banks household and suddenly this poor overworked chap is having to contend with hyperactive kids, distracted staff and talking furniture.

He's already being outmanoeuvred in his own house by women and children and now has to cope with a magic nanny he didn't employ in the first place (who, let's not forget, deployed a magic gust of wind to dispatch the other candidates in a brazen act of industrial espionage). A lesser man would have gone next door and turned that cannon on his own house but no, he's a bloke, so he sucks it up and soldiers on.

Eventually, Banks's defences lower and he gets sucked into the mania of talking furniture and show tunes, and quits his high-powered job to go and fly a fucking kite!

The Poppins purists will point out that, in the final scene, he does get his job back at the Dawes Tomes Mousley Grubbs Fidelity Fiduciary Bank, but that all feels a bit Disney. It's not how Edwardian England worked at the time. The man would've become an absolute joke in polite society. The world of high finance was in no way ready for the kind of hands-on dad who'd want time off to help his kids prep for World Book Day. So no, I don't find the ending of the film to be realistic (casually leaving aside other realism issues such as cartoon penguins and magic spoons).

I'd like to see a real-world sequel to the events of *Mary Poppins*, a gritty account of the next years in the Banks family's life as they'd have been more likely to transpire. This would be my pitch:

It's two months after Mr Banks quit his job and the family savings are starting to run out. Banks has had to let the staff go and Mrs Banks has reluctantly quit the protest scene and finally got a job.

Poor young Michael Banks has had to go cap in hand to Bert to formally take up a role as chimney sweep, which he can do thanks to the lax employment rules of the time, where he finds the jaunty songs have stopped and the hard work begins.

Eventually, the whole family starts to resent Banks as they realise they did want a more empathic father, but not at the expense of a nice lifestyle.

Maybe I'm taking it too seriously. Maybe I've now become the Mr Banks who needs a bit of saving. It's possible.

I've noticed that as I've got older, there's one bit of dialogue which always makes me emotional. Jane and Michael have been in trouble with their dad and start low level trash-talking Mr Banks to Bert, but good old Bert is having none of it and drops a couple of truth bombs. He reminds Michael of the people who keep an eye on him every day, but that there's no one keeping a similar eye out for their father and that his troubles are something he works through without complaint, 'alone' and 'silent'.

It gets me every time.

It's not right to completely dismiss the emotional message of *Mary Poppins* but we could all do with watching it again and, at the very least, accept that Mr Banks – emotionally stunted though he was – was putting in a shift and trying to do the right thing for his family. I think in the language of love it's what's called an 'act of service'.

Perhaps he did get his job back at the bank, which had suddenly become a touchy-feely organisation with beanbags and dress-down Fridays, but by God, him going cuckoo in front of the board members was one hell of a risk and frankly not the action of a responsible family man.

Motherhood can benefit from being romanticised, but fatherhood can excel when it comes to the perception of taking one for the team. That's what being a bloke is all about. Flying a kite is fun, but some days the fun is for other people, especially when there's hard graft to be done.

BLOKES NEED A MAXIMUM OF THREE HAIRSTYLES IN A LIFETIME

In one of the more extreme assertions in this book I'm going to confidently state that any bloke having more than three hairstyles in his lifetime has serious psychological problems.

I'm not throwing shade on women – who can easily go from bob, to feathered to pixie cut in the space of one crazy summer – I'm saying the rules are different for blokes. For us, changing hairstyle is more like moving house: if you do it too often you'll end up lacking any sense of where to call home.

A fella's first haircuts aren't even really his choice, or they weren't when I was growing up. While girls would petition for pigtails or ponytails, wavy or crimped, I was more or less told 'you're having a crew cut, boy'. It wasn't my mum readying me for national service, more that crew cuts were cheap or that she was happy to do them herself. While my sister's visits to the hairdressers were almost ceremonial affairs, mine had the functionality of an agricultural shearing.

The fact that my hair was cut by my mum reflected how little status it held. It was just another in a long line of highly skilled things mums feel qualified to do (thank God she was working full-time when I needed a circumcision). My mum did have a go at my sister's hair from time to time, but that all stopped the time she ended up looking like Terry from *Minder*.

The three main hairstyles of my life have been: crew cut, faux hawk and side parting. There were three shocking days in the early nineties when I had not only curtains but curls in them, like I'd swung by Madchester via a tumble dryer. It was got rid of so quickly that I consider it akin to a marriage quickly annulled.

The boldest hairstyle choice I ever made was the 'faux hawk'.

It was the early noughties. I was in my mid-twenties and had decided it was time to attract a female life partner. The way I'd do that was by having a mixture of a flat top and my hair pushed forward and a bit to the middle. It was the haircut of choice for a lot of cool blokes on telly at the time, so I felt pretty confident I'd be married within the year.

Shortly after the big rug rethink, I made the mistake of imploring a female colleague who I fancied to 'Look at my hair!'. This was overheard by a mate and the phrase 'look at my hair' is still a catchphrase on the lads' WhatsApp group.

The style was called 'faux hawk' because it looks like a mohawk for the risk averse. It was part of a trend at the time, seeded by the likes of David Beckham, in which ordinary men toyed with what was formerly uber-masculine imagery. Beckham was having the kind of macho tatts once favoured by mechanics at deserted gas stations in Utah. Consequently, blokes like me, who were not quite ready to 'get inked', settled instead for T-shirts bearing this kind of artwork. Nothing says 'manly' like tattoos which are 100 per cent machine washable.

The faux hawk was, for a time, a trendy hairstyle, and it was a real departure for me. It did the job too, as within a couple of years I actually did meet the love of my life. She didn't actually say 'amazing faux hawk let's spend the rest of our lives together' but in some ways she didn't need to.

That hairstyle lasted right up until the early 2010s. The faux hawk started to wear a bit thin on thirty-year-olds and my ever-expanding spam meant it looked like I was trying to show as much forehead cleavage as possible.

I'd already sensed my lurch towards small-c conservatism, so a side parting seemed like the next and most logical step. It was good enough for my granddad to fight the Nazis with, so it should be sufficient to guide me through my forties. I wanted the kind of immaculate side parting that would make me look like a safe bet for a twenty-five-year mortgage.

To my surprise, the new hairstyle got a bit of stick on the comedy circuit; maybe they wisely realised that as my hair became small-c conservative the rest might follow. However, one of my comedy heroes, Bob Mills, gave a more positive reaction. He said I looked like a 'Spitfire pilot' and it wasn't meant as an insult.

The side parting is where my hairstyle has stayed ever since. I'm happy here; it's like a forever home. There's nothing I can do about my receding hairline, but we're nowhere near comb-over territory. Yet. I can't grumble: my spam may be getting bigger but my hair has remained reasonably dark, just like my old man's did. His stayed dark right up until the end. He barely spent any money on his hair during an entire lifetime but died with the kind of barnet modern men would pay six grand for.

It may sound a bit fusty to have decided on a haircut for life before I turned thirty but if blokery is about consistency and a lack of fuss, there's something to be said for picking a style and bloody well sticking with it.

Look at Noel Edmonds. Following the huge success of *Noel's House Party*, he spent many years in the TV wilderness. Did he start dicking around with his rug? No. When he made his triumphant return with *Deal or no Deal*, Noel emerged with the exact same hair we'd last seen him with. What a power play!

The most respected men in society aren't changing their haircuts every other week. You'd never see George Clooney bust out a skin-fade and curtains within the same year. Or Bradley Cooper lurch between his glorious brushed-back mane and a buzz cut. And what would we conclude if Boris Johnson actually started combing his hair? That he had turned over a new leaf? Or was facing a court appearance? David Beckham was simply the exception who proved the rule.

The problem with blokes constantly messing about with their hair is it represents an admission that they give a shit. You're letting everyone know you spend a long time thinking about your appearance.

I can hear a lot of women thinking 'What's wrong with that?'

You simply can't compare men and women's attitudes to hair. There's no equivalent male phrase for 'a woman's hair is her crowning glory'. Female investment in hair is exponentially higher. I've never knowingly paid fifteen quid for shampoo. Or bought shampoo (though I'm happy to use my wife's – I see it as revenge for all the over-sized hoodies which have mysteriously gone missing).

I also found out recently that pretty much every woman I know dyes her hair. Not only that, they sometimes use mad phrases like 'I'm dying it back to its natural colour'. They've got so far lost in the hair game that they can no longer detect why 'dying' something back to its 'natural' colour could be seen as an unusual concept.

You only have to look at most blokes' attitude to going to the barbers to get a sense of how functionally we view our locks.

Most men I know baulk at the idea of making an appointment and, furthermore, if they arrive and there's more than one other bloke waiting ahead of them in the queue they'll strop out like a commuter who's just seen his next three trains cancelled.

In short, I don't want hair to be something I have to think about very often. There's far more interesting stuff going on inside my head. Ideally, I'd like to make the same monthly time investment in my hair as I do remembering to buy dog food.

IT'S PROBABLY NOTHING

Women make 50 per cent more visits to the doctors per year than men.

Recently, I had the comedian Richard Herring on my podcast talking about his experience with testicular cancer. He relayed how he'd been one of those guys who'd encouraged other men to check their balls while simultaneously failing to check his own (though thankfully he still caught it in good time). I echoed his entreaty to all men to give their balls a once over while being dimly aware that I would still fail to check my own.

Why was that? What kind of madness can allow me to fully take on board an argument while subconsciously electing to not follow its obvious wisdom?

It must be particularly weird for women who see their fella absent-mindedly fondling his bits every third minute for non-medical reasons, yet when there's finally a socially acceptable, even clinical, reason to touch his privates, he suddenly goes all coy.

On a basic level – and this may not be a common thing – I just find my balls a bit weird. The design features of the actual penis aren't too bad, but the balls are just . . . odd. These tiny hypersensitive things suspended in a sack. I guess I'm worried that I'll find a lump but also grossed out by the texture. In the same way some people get freaked out by Velcro. It's odd to have an organ which has chosen to live in such a dangerous place, like those Arctic geese who bring up their young on the edge of a cliff.

There's another reason for this blind spot, one which is perhaps more common (and less weird) than my own bollock dysmorphia: blokes just aren't as dialled into their bodies as women are.

Think about it: from the moment of that first menstrual cycle, nature gives women a regular heads-up that their body is 'doing stuff'. Men only have sporadic alerts that there's anything going on at all.

Such signals don't happen that often, full stop, and most of them are weighted towards early life in any case. You go through puberty, your voice drops, your balls drop, your body odour goes up – but once that's done . . . nothing. In fact, if you're lucky enough to experience general good health, you might go decades where your body reports that it's all quiet on the western front. Any changes that do occur generally aren't good. Hair in the nose. Hair in the ears. Hair in most places apart from the one where you want it, just as if your nose and ears are taunting your forehead.

Our bodies are less vocal than women's; consequently, we have the scope to ignore any of the weird shit taking place within. It will often take high levels of discomfort before we even consider taking action.

My dad was a real martyr in this respect.

When he was in his early sixties, my sister invited my dad out to Houston for a holiday and treated him to a pedicure. Not long after she'd started, the woman performing the treatment looked up in concern, in much the same way a surgeon might glance around if an operation was going wrong. They'd noticed my dad had a very serious in-growing toenail. When questioned about it, Dad cheerfully reported back that he'd had it for about ten years. He elaborated that, rather than go to the doctors, he'd instead opted to periodically 'dig it out' himself.

The employees of the spa looked baffled.

However, for my dad, properly attending to his toenail would create a fuss, and on a daily basis the physical discomfort was preferrable to fuss. He got up every single day and compared the niggling pain in his foot to the ball ache of visiting a doctor. Every single day, he weighed up the pros and cons then came down on the side of going about his business as usual. If he'd have just teased out his logic a little and plotted another graph he might've compared overall loss of quality of life versus localised inconvenience, but that wasn't how my dad's mind worked.

I guess the further it went the more embarrassed he became. He knew he'd have to undergo the ignominy of whoever worked on his feet pulling out an industrial-sized planer while shielding their face with a welder's mask to avoid potentially lethal shards of toenail. Even so, it's undeniable that once ten years had passed, a quick visit to the doctors and the attendant treatment would've been better than the day-in, day-out soreness, but the old man took a gamble and on one level I respect that – partly because the apple doesn't fall far from the tree.

In the mid-noughties I got a verruca. I'd had it about a year and thought I should probably mention it to my wife, who suggested a bunch of things which sounded like a massive pain in the arse, so I googled what to do.

I found one article which suggested that the best thing to do was to just leave it.

So I did.

Don't get me wrong, there were plenty of other articles suggesting all manner of treatments, including freezing part of my foot and making various dietary adjustments involving almonds, but I opted to observe the one article I found which allowed me to do sod all.

That verruca became a part of me for ten whole years. Whenever it came up my wife renewed her petitions for me to get it seen to, but I claimed that, as I'd taken it this far, it was probably only days from resolving itself.

But here's the thing. One day, that verruca did resolve itself. One magical, blessed morning I checked the bottom of my foot and it had just disappeared. Probably the worst thing that can happen to an avoidant man like me is that I invent some logically dubious basis for postponement which gets proved correct, but only by good luck and the passing of time.

Since then, I've had other stuff which I left for ten years.

In 2010 I was told that I might need glasses. Ten short years later, I got my first pair of glasses and suffered multiple panic attacks when I realised I'd driven nearly half a million miles seeing life with all the visual clarity of old episodes of *The Simpsons* on Channel 4. I don't know what had stopped me from getting glasses. Did I think Specsavers were somehow lying to me? That they operated like cowboy mechanics, recommending a new cambelt I didn't need? Did I think my driving was so good I could basically get around Britain like a Jedi using the Force?

I currently have bunions on my feet. 'Get it checked out, Geoff,' my wife says.

Why? I've only had them four years. With such matters you need to give it at least another six before considering action. Anything less would seem hasty.

What can also be particularly maddening for women is that, in most areas, blokes generally aren't as fussed by their own physical discomfort. It simply doesn't register as highly on our personal Richter scale of things to give a shit about.

Sometimes I'll slump on the couch in a visibly piss-poor posture. My wife will cajole me to rearrange the pillows. 'Get up and sort yourself out, Geoff,' she'll say, 'you'll be more comfortable.'

Nonsense! I'll just ride out the lower back pain and grow as a person. Many women will watch men sitting or doing something in a cack-handed way and offer to help. We don't always want help. We don't know what we want, but we do know that we don't want fuss. Fuss is a pain, fuss is un-British, but most of all, fuss is un-blokey.

I'm not saying that all this is necessarily a good thing. As much as I'm amused by stoicism I recognise the need for change. Due to the way humans procreate, men are literally the place where evolution is – or should be – happening (maybe that's why I'm so freaked out by my balls – it's a lot of responsibility).

So we need to try to learn how to reach out for help.

But how do you pitch this to a meat-and-two-veg guy, steadfastly ignoring back pain or peculiar sensations in his chest?

Well, if making a fuss is the concern, a bloke dying needlessly young could be seen to be the epitome of fuss. Maybe that's the way to sell the idea of intervention to men with chronic white-coat syndrome. There would be a funeral to plan, people would have to take time off work (because for some bloody reason these things have to happen during office hours), there would be free food for relatives you're not fond of, and – worst of all – the bloody admin.

So maybe that's how you need to pitch a doctor's visit to the bloke in your life. Point out the potential lost earnings, the fact coffins are only single use (you're literally throwing money away, like when you drive a brand-new motor off the forecourt). Then hit him with the clincher, the worst of all these things: the criminal price of buffets.

He'll be down the quack's like a shot.

Aside: Since I wrote this chapter, my sister has clarified that my dad went ahead with the pedicure. Afterwards he was borderline euphoric, commenting that it was 'like walking on someone else's feet'. Not that he ever had one again, mind, which is classic blokery.

ARMCHAIR GENERALS

'I hated Hitler growing up but as I've got older, I realised without him I wouldn't have had as many good documentaries to watch.'

– *Geoff Norcott Snr, 2013*

There are some things which eventually come to all blokes over time. As a young man, you think that you'll be immune to the standard and clichéd interests of your forefathers, but in time these things call out to you like sirens of tedium: strong cheese, trains, peace and quiet, socks which don't make your feet too hot.

And, above all these, stands the enduring appeal of the Second World War.

For a certain generation of dads, the History Channel (or the 'Hitler Channel' as it affectionately became known) launched at exactly the right time. A lot of fellas from that era were retiring and the standard daytime televisual fare of talking women and gameshows didn't hold much interest. But the History Channel? Suddenly they could spend whole days immersed in the twentieth century's most re-tellable tale.

Before Channel 5 got lost in making the same royal documentary with a thousand different titles, the History Channel was doing the same with Hitler. *Hunting Hitler, The Rise of Adolf Hitler, Hitler's Legacy of Death, Hitler and the Order of the Phoenix* (I may have made the last one up). I used to mock my dad for how long he'd spend glued to these shows. It seemed like he was watching a replay of the same event from a million different angles (which, given modern sports coverage, is not entirely outside the blokey frame of interest).

At school, I'd had that first wave of interest in the Second World War that most boys experience. At that age, the appeal is obvious: primarily that England won (sorry, Britain won . . . Sorry, Britain and America . . . Sorry. Britain and *how many* countries?). I was aware of the big moments, the key figures and, on a basic level, the evils perpetrated by the Nazis, but as I became an adult man, like most blokes, I filed all that away for a while.

My, how things have changed lately. I don't know when I realised I'd become a Second World War guy. It might've been when I started listening to numerous podcasts on the subject and it became the only new information I had to relay to my wife. Over the course of a twenty-year marriage, I'd used up all my decent anecdotes, but what I could now do was regale her with exciting trivia about the war. Like, did she know that, during the war, Himmler once turned up in Britain unannounced? Was she aware how much Hitler detested smoking? And did she know that the name of the bomber which dropped the first H-bomb was 'Enola Gay'?

You're right. She *is* a lucky girl. It's the kind of thing any woman in a long marriage wants to hear on a rare date night.

'Would you like to see the vegetarian menu, Geoff?'

'No . . . but I'll tell you who else was a vegetarian.'

What's peculiar about Second World War history is that the more I aged the more it started to seem recent. I was born in 1976, only thirty years after the end of the war. My mum used to take me to the Imperial War Museum in London when I was small, but back then it all seemed like ancient history. When

114

you're ten, forty years ago is four times your lifetime. By the time you're forty, something that happened eighty years ago is down to only double the time you've been alive.

Something else that happens as you age is that the concept of time is something you start bending to your will. To stop yourself feeling too old, the mind reflexively recalibrates your view of all history as less distant. Thatcher? Left office recently, didn't she? Second World War? It is closer to my birth year than we are now to the TV debut of *Mr Bean*. The pyramids? Surely they were built shortly before work was completed on the Elizabeth line.

Thinking of the Second World War as more recent also helps make it feel more real. It becomes less heroic and more a human endeavour that you have to try to get your head around.

The move from it seeming like something mythic to a real-life event made me go back over the inane questions I once asked my grandfather (who served in North Africa). As a boy, I asked him things I now regret, like did he drive a tank? Did he ever meet Churchill? And whether or not he shot anyone. If he was still alive today he'd probably shoot himself, such would be the wealth of info I'd be mining him for.

When I asked my grandfather those questions I had a simplistic sense of goodies versus baddies. As you age, you realise that few things can be delineated so comfortably. Most historical conflicts have two complicated sides. You even rewatch *Star Wars* thinking, 'Well, I don't like the way they went about it, but the Galactic Empire weren't entirely wrong about streamlining the clunking bureaucracy of the Old Republic.'

The Second World War, on the other hand – with some small caveats – does fall more easily into a classic sense of 'Jedi versus Sith'. You can talk with nuance about the effect of the Treaty of

Versailles in provoking the conflict, and the degree of culpability of the German people, but the Nazi high command were demonstrably evil. The things carried out in their name mean that no reasonable person could wish for anything other than an Allied victory.

The degree to which you celebrate or own this moral victory can be the tricky thing. In recent times, there's been a legitimate criticism of the boomer generation for constantly invoking a war they never actually fought in. Triumphalism is intrinsic to sport so there's always a risk that blokes can start connecting those same emotions to the war.

However, I suspect that when British blokes look back to the war, the defining part of the national story isn't drawn from heroism. Sure there's the Dam Busters, but is that about the mission itself or a cracking theme tune? There's the Battle of Britain, but all that aerial combat stuff is so elegant that it seems completely removed from the gritty reality of boots-on-the-ground combat. The things that really stick in the mind are the narrow escapes. Dunkirk is a far more meaningful analogy. As any football fan knows, winning 5–0 is so euphoric it feels almost otherworldly, but scraping a last-minute equaliser is where the true exhilaration lies. As a cricket fan, my most cherished memory isn't beating the Aussies at home 3–0, or bigger still winning down under, it's from 2009 when our two worst batters somehow survived twenty overs to bat out for an unlikely draw.

Stubbornness is often associated with blokes and what could be more downright bloody-minded than withstanding the Blitz? Those years were rarely about obvious acts of courage; it was men and women exhibiting bravery of a different kind. The bravery of just getting on with it and not giving in. Far from

British exceptionalism, these obdurate tales are the narratives which actually form our national character. The average bloke absolutely loves this stuff.

My son is already aware of the basic tenets of the war, but I wonder if the passage of time might ultimately mean his interest will exist on a much lower level than mine. It seems logical that it would. Mine might be the last generation to get so lost in the fact and mythology of the Second World War.

And there's a material reason so many of my contemporaries are still hooked: because so many men fought in the war, there remains a palpable link in its effect on the relationships between fathers and sons. My granddad came back from the war still a lovely human being, but troubled. My dad spent the first few years of his life without a father figure present and, when granddad was about, he had a lot on his mind. Consequently, the bond between them took a long time to recover. It affected how my dad would one day parent me.

All of which is a heavily convoluted way of saying I'm probably going to consume Second World War stuff until I die – and also that my dad never took me fishing and it's all Hitler's fault.

SPORTING HOLY TRINITY #2: CRICKET

It's hard to make an argument that Test cricket is quintessentially blokey when the numbers don't back up the sport's broad appeal. Once when I was appearing on *Pointless Celebrities*, the host asked us which young celebrities we thought the public would've heard of. On the board were people like Maya Jama, some chirpy bloke off *I'm a Celebrity*, and England captain Ben Stokes. I concluded that – given his lion heart and gargantuan achievements out in the middle – pretty much everyone would've heard of Ben Stokes, so I tried to get a low score by picking some funky dude from Radio 1.

It turned out that only 13 per cent of the general public asked knew who Ben Stokes was. Thirteen per cent? The Hero of Headingley? The Lion of Lords? Less famous than Maya Jama? (No shade on Maya but I don't remember her more or less single-handedly winning the ODI World Cup). So the purpose of this chapter is to convince the majority of blokes that they're missing out on a sport which is perfect for them. I'm taking a liberty with its inclusion, so let's see if I can win anyone over.

Not only do most people not like cricket, they seem to savour their antipathy, even though that's the majority position (similar to people who seem to want credit for telling you they don't like U2 or have never watched *Star Wars*). I can understand the superficial reasons so many blokes tend towards football rather than Test cricket. It doesn't make me angry – I just feel sorry for them. I'm not certain of many things in this life, but I am sure that Test cricket is one of mankind's greatest achievements.

I came to the sport at the best time possible, at England's absolute nadir. We were spending yet another summer getting beaten up by the all-conquering Aussies, to the point where even small achievements felt like big wins. One of our tail-enders, John Embury, scored a quick-fire fifty in a losing cause and was heralded like he'd found a cure for cancer.

Cricket is unique in that people who aren't in the team for batting still have to bat. In football, if a goalkeeper goes up for a last-minute corner it's normally out of desperation. If a striker goes in goal it might be because the keeper headbutted someone and got a red card. In cricket, however, this 'Freaky Friday' role changing isn't just an occasional one-off – it's woven into the fabric of the sport. The scope this creates for blokey banter is huge. A tail-ender who can't bat for toffee facing a world-class bowler at 90mph will pull people from the bars. He's either going to get hit in the balls or launch the other fella into the stands.

There couldn't be a more unlikely hero than someone like Jack Leach, a slow bowler who stood at the other end while Ben Stokes was performing his 2019 heroics. Leach faced seventeen balls for his solitary run, but the way he held up one end for the guy with the talent was the epitome of solid blokery. He even managed to throw in a comedy run-out chance when a kamikaze attempt for a single had him scrambling back to the other end.

Ben Stokes couldn't even watch when Leach was facing, and

spent almost all of his team-mate's seventeen balls on his haunches with his eyes covered.

When Jack did eventually score his solitary run it was with near comical nonchalance. Having ducked and dived the previous sixteen, Leach casually tucked the ball off his hip to tie the Test match. Like going on a stag-do and your weediest mate throwing the most powerful right hook on the arcade punch machine.

Another charge made against cricket's masculine credentials is that it's not very manly. It's an accusation often made by football fans, who, let's not forget, routinely watch multi-millionaires get taken out by a random gust of wind. And yet, in cricket, a rock-hard ball is propelled at your head at speeds which would attract six points on your licence. Admittedly, cricket can seem a bit limp at times as they do stop for a nice lunch . . . and afternoon tea . . . and yes, they do sometimes stop playing because it's a bit dark or drizzly, but when the real action gets down to business it's as replete with physical jeopardy as anything Formula 1 has to offer.

As a sport, cricket also boasts many features blokes tend to be drawn towards. It's got stats (I could quickly rattle off the batting averages of several players who retired when John Major was still in charge). There's also duration. If some of sport's appeal to blokes is about switching off, note that football is only ninety minutes; Test cricket is five. Whole. Days.

That's why me and my mates have made it an annual trip for so many years now. It's just more time watching sport.

In 2022, I went to see England versus New Zealand at Headingly. I arrived at ten in the morning and didn't leave until

6pm. That's just good value, plus we were well oiled and sporting a decent tan (we even applied sun cream that day).

However, this was post pandemic and I hadn't accounted for how much older we'd got in the intervening two years. Something terrible happened on our first post-Covid cricket day.

One of our mates had a little snooze during the afternoon session.

It was that nightmare image I'd seen for years, the one when, during a lull in play, the cameras would drift to an old duffer catching forty winks under the cover of a wide-brimmed hat. I'd always pitied those guys. Nothing makes a bloke look quite so old and worn out as falling asleep during the day, especially when so many recreational activities are within arm's reach. Imagine being so old that though there is the option of playing crowd beach ball or watching cricket, you instead elect to have a little sleep. There was a beer snake going on not twenty yards away.

If you don't know what a 'beer snake' is, I believe it represents the high watermark of blokey bollocks. As people drink beer throughout a day of cricket, an ocean of plastic pint glasses builds up in the seating area. Eventually – and I've never caught sight of the visionary who starts this process – some bloke will start collecting all the cups and stacking them one on top of another. I don't know if he starts out with genuine good intentions – maybe he's into recycling or helping the ground staff control the litter – but it starts to grow in length and becomes 'the snake'. Blokes from far and wide start running towards the snake to add to it. There's a weird shamanic chant which starts up, where people repeat the entreaty to *'Feed the snake, Feed the snake'*.

The snake quickly becomes more important than the cricket

and the need for its perpetual growth becomes an all-consuming focus. My wife rang me once to talk about important plans for the weekend, but I cut the call short, saying, 'Babe, can I call back? We're feeding the snake!'

She sent me a follow-up text, asking, 'What the fuck is the snake?' It was a fair question, particularly as it sounded like a euphemism for something sexual.

When I got home the following day I explained to her what the snake was and that our one had got so big that Sky had covered it between deliveries. No less than Michael Vaughan had expressed his admiration.

I think that explanation was worse than any of the potential answers she'd come up with in the meantime.

Test cricket gets its name for a reason: it goes on so long it can test the psyche. A 6–0 defeat in football or a hammering in rugby is at least over quickly. Defeat in a five-Test series is a soul-sapping examination of character. The duration also provides the sport with a depth which others struggle to match. The rivalries across a five-match series spanning several months can be epic. Consequently, some of the insults – or 'sledges' – have been so rich they've gone into folklore.

Jimmy Ormond was playing for England against an Australia team which contained the Waugh brothers: Mark and the more highly rated Steve. Mark Waugh commented that Jimmy wasn't good enough to play for England, to which Ormond replied, 'Maybe not, but at least I'm the best player in my family.'

Football is great, but the birthplace for such linguistic highlights as 'over the moon' isn't known for such withering put-downs.

Even the on-tour high jinx operate on a different level.

Football scandals are often a bit route one and sometimes very unsavoury. I don't know if a footballer has ever done anything as eccentric as borrowing a biplane to fly over the field his team-mates were playing on while the game happened (doffs cap to David Gower), or as comically goofy as Freddie Flintoff nicking a pedalo to try to join a party on a yacht. Cricket anecdotes often go down in folklore, while football ones can end up in court.

Amid an increasingly rapid digestion of entertainment and sport, Test cricket is a stay against confusion. Is the duration such a problem? At a time when people routinely devour six series boxsets perhaps it still has a place.

And if all that hasn't sold you, let me say this: Test cricket is a place where you can have a beer in your hand before 11am and literally no one thinks it's weird.

You're welcome.

MAN FLU

'Man flu is a pejorative phrase which refers to the idea that men, when they have a common cold, experience and self-report symptoms of greater severity, akin to those experienced during the flu. However, there is evidence to suggest that viral infections affect men more than women.'

– *Wikipedia*

OK, so there it is. Wikipedia says that man flu is real so I guess we can finally stop arguing about it?

Perhaps not . . .

When it comes to illness, let's be honest and say that the average bloke's relationship with illness has changed over the years. If your great-granddad caught rickets or got winged by a stray shot from a musket, he'd still insist on doing his duty and going to work – even if he had to crawl on his calcium-deficient knees to get there. Bed was a place where he slept at night and procreated twice in a lifetime, not somewhere to spend time during the day under any circumstances.

Even worse, if he were to admit that he felt a bit under the weather it would lead to the ultimate nightmare scenario: women making a fuss.

Even if blokes have become less resilient over time, man flu is a contentious idea because it brings into play two strong and opposing forces: women, who, on the whole, don't really like hearing men moan about stuff, versus men, who claim to not like moaning but moan a lot when ill.

Whether there are sound biological reasons why man flu is a real thing or not, whining is never a good look for a bloke. We act like big kids often enough as it is.

But why do blokes become so moany when ill? When men have an infection or virus, testosterone levels decrease as the body redeploys energy to fight off the bug. This might be a reason why ill blokes whinge so much – because there's been a temporary reduction in the flow of that weapons-grade hormone which allows us to thrust and fight (or at the very least make a bold move for the last parking space). Not only are we ill, we feel biologically and emotionally weaker. The science is all there.

During the pandemic, men were 61 per cent more likely to die from Covid-19, but even this wasn't enough to spotlight the idea that men might suffer more acutely.

If that had been reversed and women had been more likely to die, I've no doubt there'd have been a UN commission on the subject and Emma Watson would've been wearing a tasteful ribbon bearing the numbers '61' – but, in the event, the disparity in Covid deaths warranted relatively little in the way of column inches.

Without sounding flippant, the pandemic gave the average bloke a new card to play. His Mrs may have been suspicious of the man-flu claims, but the idea it might be Covid had to be taken seriously. It was a risky move, however, because eventually he'd have to take the test – then try to sound convincing when claiming that he 'must have shaken it off already'. (Not that I was any good at taking those tests. It took me about five attempts before I even reached where my tonsils used to be. My wife said it was worse than giving tablets to the dog.)

At a time when we've become suspicious of toxic traits like victim-blaming, the idea of 'man flu' sails very close to the idea of 'gaslighting'. You tell someone something's wrong and they tell you it's all in your mind.

There's something minimising about putting the word 'man' in front of an ailment in order to undermine it. We're one step away from hearing things like, 'Oh, you've got man-kidney stones have you? I'm sure they're *very* man-painful.' On the one hand, men are being exhorted that they need to 'talk more' and learn to be comfortable with seeming vulnerable. On the other, domestically, many are still being told to 'stop moaning'. So essentially, it seems like we need to speak up, but quietly, and definitely not when we're ill.

My advice for blokes dealing with this quandary is itself very blokey: deal with it. Suck it up. Women will always be a little bit suspicious of the idea that you contracted the exact same cold as them but that, somehow the moment it got in your body it became a vicious brand of flu. It's like sitting next to someone on the very same mobile network with the identical phone yet declaring you have worse signal. And that's before you throw in the fact that the very concept of pain is a bone of contention in any marriage, especially one which has produced children. You may have a paper cut on your finger that stings like a bastard or a blister from wearing new shoes that has made your heel feel like it's on fire, but if you ask your wife for sympathy you are asking the wrong question. If you do want sympathy put that poorly finger in a sling and hobble your aching foot down to the pub where other men will feel your pain and show their empathy by cutting up your peanuts for you and gently trickling lager down your throat. And they will do all that for the simple reason that they've never given birth.

If you want the women around you to take your illness seriously, it's worth doing a bit of soldiering on. Let it get to a point where they independently realise you're more ill than you're letting on. That way, you'll finally get a bit of sympathy which is turbo-charged by their guilt for not taking you at face value in the first place (this can be a risky tactic – 'soldiering on' should never include 'missing chemo').

But you need to do something because it will never come down to simply how ill you *say* you are. Women are far more shrewd and tuned in to your usual behaviours than you are to theirs. They need to see concrete evidence on top of your own verbal reports (which may be a painfully transparent attempt to get out of attending their mum's sixtieth).

Blokes don't clock minor deviations in their other half's behaviour in quite the same way. It doesn't only happen with physical health; women can log a wide range of changes in behaviour (or they've simply mastered the magical art of 'paying attention'). They're making decisions based on a more rounded understanding of who we are. Consequently, a bloke exhibiting small behavioural changes can indeed make them take notice.

For example, I like my food. In forty-six years of life, I've had my full complement of three daily meals on every single day bar two. I like food so much that I try to eat lunch as late as possible, so I have more of the day with lunch still to look forward to. After dinner, I'll often leave pudding a good ninety minutes, so I have fewer waking hours where food isn't a prospect. So if I ever leave food on the plate, or even turn down an extra helping of mashed potato, my wife will often shoot me the same kind of worried look a zoo keeper gives a penguin who's off his fish.

So what can we conclude? That I have an odd relationship with food which stems from being breastfed for too long? Probably. However, more importantly, if I'm under the weather, me not eating is a more convincing sign of illness than whatever whiny claims I make. Women are great at playing the long game. Sometimes we should too.

And given that blokes seem to have done OK in the 'biological burden' tally chart, perhaps we just need to accept the irony that testosterone – as well as often being hostile to everything else – is also destructive to men's immune system. It can make us crash economies and start wars, but might also cause our immune system to occasionally annexe itself. But as we don't have to give birth or go through the menopause, maybe we can take this one for the team (if anything, our female partner's ability to grow additional hair in late middle age is something we might end up feeling jealous of).

Conversely, oestrogen can be friendly to the immune system. Surprise, surprise, the hormone most associated with being biologically female has the power to co-operate. I suspect oestrogen also remembers to send adrenaline a card on its birthday.

And if you, as a bloke, feel really ill and you want to go super-radical to get your wife or girlfriend's attention, you could take truly radical action, like, I dunno, booking a doctor's appointment.

IT'S JUST A BLUR ON A SCREEN

*The average age at which British men become
a father is 33.7.*

From conception to delivery, it's sobering to consider the pitiful
scale of blokes' involvement in pregnancy.

The average man at any given point carries enough sperm in
his testicles to impregnate if not the whole of Europe, then at least
halfway from Britain to Bulgaria.

An average woman, however, hits puberty with just enough
eggs to populate a decent-sized British city.

Like many aspects of maleness, that statistical potential is not
something blokes generally deliver on. If you take an average
British bloke who sires two kids in his life and reduce the equation
to the amount of times he had sex (5,778 for British men . . . I'm
thinking that graph skews heavily between the ages of 18 and 30)
then he has ejaculated the potential for many times the earth's
population. After all that semen, two kids is a fairly meagre
return. Most blokes like to think they're Harry Kane, but in the
fertility stakes, we're barely Emile Heskey.

Nature constantly hints that life and creation revolves
around women. All the most important things are round: eggs,
planets, suns, orbits . . . boobs. It's why men are so obsessed
with curves, because we know that without them the universe
simply doesn't work.

If we take the average duration of British sex (nineteen minutes in total, with nine of those for actual sex . . . again, I'm seeing another graph spiking heavily between ages 18 and 30) and compare that to the number of minutes pregnancy lasts across nine months, we find that the physical male investment in pregnancy and gestation is 0.00000000025 per cent of the woman's.

The real miracle about fatherhood – given that we don't carry the child or have any kind of tactile relationship throughout pregnancy – is how so many men are actively engaged in the first months after the child is born. Up until that point, the whole process might have felt a bit theoretical.

The physical burden of pregnancy falls exclusively on the woman, but the state of pregnancy is at least a tangible reality, with changes in her body and mood – plus she'll probably feel the baby move regularly. The man will be told about all of these things and in the case of mood, may see evidence of them as another plant pot goes flying past his head. But still, the whole project remains fairly abstract throughout gestation.

Even the first scan shows a human form which looks nothing like a human, via an ultrasound method that seems better suited to detecting submarines. You hold your wife's hand meaningfully and do your best simpering look, but the logical part of your brain is bugged by the poor picture and feels like you should check that the HDMI cable is in properly.

After that first scan, there's a long stretch when there's little else in the way of new evidence that this miracle is actually happening.

The second trimester passes and, for a lot of couples, things are pretty benevolent. She has a bump which seems to be a size and shape she's happy to show off. In many cases, her mood is good;

you see the glow you'd heard so much about, which is frequently just her feeling hot, but you take the wins where you can.

Then, right at the very end of this miraculous nine-month process, you see the first incontrovertible evidence of the process as your child is finally born. And it is a truly amazing moment. When my son emerged and took his first breath in the form of a cry the words 'oh God' slipped out of my mouth, in a moment of spontaneous spirituality.

Or maybe it was me thinking, 'Oh God, how am I going to feed and clothe this thing?' or 'Oh God, that's a *lot* of fluid.'

To this day, the sound of him crying always makes me smile because it remains the greatest sound I've ever heard. It was his first noise in the world, the first evidence he was OK, the first hurdle of being alive passed – the keenest gratitude I've ever known.

It must be weird for my son – every time he has a fall or grazes his shin, I'll be happily cleaning the cut to the music of his tears, letting him know it all 'Takes me back to the best day of my life.'

One of the least blokey things about me is how sentimental I am as a dad. Of my wife and I, it was me who had to work hardest to keep their shit together on my son's first day at school. I tear up in the big moments. Watching *Modern Family*, I'd always presumed I'd be the whisky-sipping patriarch Jay Pritchett but I'm much closer to the mollycoddling sap Phil Dunphy.

I still have my red lines, however. When my son was a baby I couldn't do the papoose thing. I tried, but have you ever put on a single item of clothing and felt like 40 per cent of your dignity instantly disappeared?

There's a certain bloke for whom wearing papooses does work: the hipster guy with his top-knot, long-sleeve white T-shirt and pastel-coloured long johns. I'm sure guys called 'Caleb' can strap on a papoose using the same evolved emotional state which allows them not to laugh at the words 'house husband'. But I generally wear polo shirts and jeans. To quote some social media feedback after an appearance on *The Mash Report*, 'Geoff looks like the kind of bloke who spends his weekend defending statues.' So if you saw me wearing a papoose you'd be far more likely to think I might have stolen that baby.

But, since I didn't want to miss out on the proximity with my boy, I decided to carry him everywhere. Carrying him all the time caused big problems with my wrists. To the point where I eventually needed surgery. I have a scar on my hand from the resultant operation. As I always tell my son, some people have tattoos to commemorate becoming a parent; I have a scar from carrying him everywhere because wearing a papoose made me feel like a lady.

Every generation of children grows up confused; I'm just finding my own unique things for my son to talk about during therapy.

One bit of good news for blokes is that we get loads of credit for doing simple acts of parenting. Be honest, when you see a dad loading two kids into a car and strapping them in you smile, right? Look at that hero! (Doing things which actually represent a legal obligation.)

When I took my son to Costa when he was a toddler, I'd notice that as I put him in the highchair and gave the surface a wipe down, there would be several middle-aged mums looking at me like they were witnessing something halfway between parenting and domestic porn. I'd get a different look off the older women, though, no doubt because their experience of raising a child saw much less in the way of male help. They'd look bewildered, almost angry, as they stared at me – like they'd witnessed a chimpanzee using hair straighteners.

I'm not saying that all modern men contribute fully but many more get stuck in than they used to. Fatherhood has evolved a lot within the space of a single generation. Even when I was growing up in the eighties, many men didn't expect to play a particularly active role in their children's lives. For some, the overwhelming responsibility of fatherhood was enough to make them abscond altogether. Dads 'doing a runner' was a familiar development.

'Heard about Terry? He's done a runner.'

'Done a runner' could mean a lot of things. It often meant moving to a different bit of Britain. Without mobiles or social media, men who were terrified by the responsibility of being a dad could piss off and live a lonely but quiet life in Norfolk. Today, women talk about being ghosted by men they've dated, but back then some men would ghost whole families. One day, many years later, their kids might be on holiday in Yarmouth, watching telly in their hotel room, then spy a familiar face behind a news reporter – 'Mum, is that *Dad* on Anglia News?'

Recently, I saw a viral TikTok of a male cat being brought into contact with one of its offspring, a small, mewling tabby kitten. The very presence of this kitten immediately activates the cat's gag reflex. The animal may have boaked for reasons other than the crushing pressure of fatherhood, but this cat retching at the mere idea of having a kid was held up as an analogy for how men react to becoming fathers. We go on to see the next stages of the cat's relationship with this kitten. It moves from that initial sickened response to a state of passive indifference, to finally being a hands-on dad (which in the cat world means occasionally licking the thing's head).

I'd like to think the success of that clip lies in the acknowledgement that, for many men, the idea of fatherhood doesn't come easy. I'm not saying it's simple for women either, but they have a head start on the tactile relationship between parent and offspring. Blokes are visual creatures and the first time we truly know we have a child to care for is when we see it right in front of us.

So, as well as being hot on the heels of bad and absent fathers, let's stop and reflect on all the blokes who – despite their flaws, limited role in childbirth and general sense of bemusement at the whole affair – stick around and try their best. Though many men initially retch like a distressed tomcat, in the end, the vast majority of us slowly but surely adjust to the role, even learning to enjoy the odd spot of paternal head-licking.

THE NEWS AT MEN

Long ago – and by 'long ago', I mean roughly 2008 – before news was something you could consume more or less constantly via the highly reliable filter of social media, there was a curious ritual men would engage in on the first day of a holiday.

On the first morning of a standard package break in the Med you'd see a familiar scene unfold. The wife would settle in for a decent shift of sunbathing, doing that mad thing you're supposed to do on holiday: relaxing. The bloke, however, would immediately look bored and twitchy. Eventually, after twenty minutes of fidgeting like a fed-up teenager who'd been coerced into that painful last holiday with his folks, he'd put his flip-flops back on and set off on a mission.

About forty-five minutes later, you'd see him return to the poolside looking pleased with himself, as he had a tabloid newspaper tucked neatly under his arm, exhibiting the pride and satisfaction once exhibited by hunters who'd caught prey.

He was happy. He'd found news. In an age when most things were freely available, news was the one thing he still had to hunt for. The 'kill' might not contain any sustenance, but he would be able to devour the results from last night's League Cup quarter-finals.

I was like this. Faced with the prospect of seven days away, I couldn't fully relax until I knew there was a reliable newspaper vendor nearby. It's an odd compulsion, as one of the purposes of a holiday is to escape from the depressing features of your normal life. Yet there I was on a beach in Malta looking at crystal blue water, azure skies and a sun unimpeded by clouds, but all I could think about was whether I could get a copy of the *Sun*. When I first started going on package holidays, before technology improved and overseas printing facilities made papers more freely available, the newspapers I did buy were often at least a day behind the ones back home. The news I was reading wasn't even new, but that didn't matter. I felt like some old emissary of the British Empire being kept abreast of developments in far-flung corners of the world by despatch riders who'd taken days to reach me.

'Your grace, Gazza has been found paraletic in another dodgy nightclub. And Debbie from Romford is still 36-24-36.'

As my holidays improved, and I went on more business trips, my overseas news consumption evolved because I could now watch it on the telly. The decent hotels often had Sky News and if they didn't, I'd watch CNN. The news didn't even have to be *my* news, just *some* news in a language I could understand. Even if I couldn't understand everything, I'd still give French news a go, which was fine, so long as the anchors were telling me their name, age and whether or not they enjoyed playing football dans le park avec their amis.

As far as I can tell, this news obsession does seem to be more of a blokey thing. That's not to say my female associates aren't interested in current affairs; they're just less interested and less often – certainly not when there's a pool nearby. They tend to devote their energy for detail to things much more immediate. That's why they're the first to notice that your child has pissed in the shallow end.

The news addiction gets worse for blokes as we stumble into middle age. As well as keeping up with the headlines, I've also developed an odd portfolio of global markets I check in on each and every day.

One is the price of crude oil (you're right, I *am* great fun on holidays). It all started after the credit crunch. As a club comic at the time, doing around 50,000 miles a year (sorry, Greta), the cost of petrol was my single biggest overhead. One unexpected consequence of all these banks going up the spout was that the price of crude oil collapsed. Then mortgages became a lot cheaper. So, in what was supposed to be the worst economic catastrophe for a generation, I was finally able to cut back on the supply teaching.

Just when I thought I could give up on checking the crude oil price, Russia invaded Ukraine. Once again, I'm checking those numbers twice a day, not to mention I've since added another habit into the mix: the gas futures index.

I also check the 'markets' continually. No idea why, it just feels like a grown-up, blokey thing to do (and a bit like I'm one of the sons in *Succession*).

This could be a problematic thing to say as it carries certain implications, but news does seem to skew blokey. Why is that? I guess knowing about worldly matters makes a bloke feel more important (superficial and easily forgotten though that information may be). It services the latter of those two key pillars of the blokey constitution: provide and protect.

We know that in the modern world the physical element of protection is rarely called upon, but that particular part of our mammal brain is still roughly the same size, so it draws other 'risks' into that space which often aren't worthy of the name. We might not be required to beat off a team of marauding scavengers, but we can engage that synapse by getting needlessly worried about a bloodless coup in Guatemala.

My dad, even in his last days, exhibited this exact trait. In the twilight of his life, despite being a trade union man, he opened a few share funds. He became quite obsessive about them, particularly after retirement, when there are several voids men need to fill.

He'd been very poorly for a while and the doctors warned us the end was nigh. One night, I was staying at his house keeping vigil. I was sleeping upstairs in my old bedroom in a bunk bed that was far too small (even for an average-sized UK male).

I heard a clatter downstairs and feared the worst. I sped down and went into the lounge, only to find my old man in his pants with his laptop open in front of him, staring at the screen.

I asked him, 'What are you doing?'

He looked at me like I was the mental one. 'I'm checking on my Prudential share fund is what I'm doing. There's been some ruckus in Bangladesh . . . what are YOU doing?'

I paused, because dads, in a moment of such madness, still get to act like the sensible ones.

He shrugged like I'd never really understood such things and said, 'Go to bed, Geoffrey, you prat.'

I trudged upstairs like the eight-year-old boy I was when I'd last lived in that house, knowing that, even in the last moments of his life, dad's word was final.

I'd also come to learn that one day I too would need to know what the hell was happening in far-off places for reasons I'd never be able to fully explain. I'm just glad my dad wasn't around when Twitter became a go-to place for news and world events. He'd have never left the house.

HEROES OF BLOKEDOM #3: BOB MORTIMER

There are some people who if you found out they were arseholes, you might just top yourself.

Into that category first I'd put Tom Hanks. If a video emerged of Tom harassing a junior assistant or drop-kicking a hamster I think humanity would be well justified in finally giving up. We might also consider throwing in the towel if it transpired that David Attenborough hated insects and 'only spoke all that nature bollocks for the wedge'. Or if it turned out that Martin Lewis doesn't in fact change his energy tariffs twice a month.

I think the same is true of Bob Mortimer.

Bob's journey towards national treasure status has been an unusual one. In his double act with Vic Reeves he was never the junior creative partner, but the fact that the first big TV show they did together was called *Vic Reeves' Big Night Out* insinuated that Bob was a sidekick when he was anything but. Anyone who watched Reeves and Mortimer shows throughout the nineties and noughties wouldn't have come away thinking that Bob was anything less than an equal partner in their act.

The thing that seemed to tip him into the category of national treasure was the moment he did stuff on his own. There were the now legendary appearances on *Would I Lie to You?*, where Bob's naturally tangential mind produced those rare moments where the 'cry laugh' emoji felt genuinely merited.

But if you need your top blokes to be not just a laugh, but also good humans, you should know that Bob did legal aid work as a lawyer and seems to be one of those people who gets on with being virtuous rather than tweeting about it.

I don't know Bob personally, but I know that everyone who's worked with him only has good things to say – but why is that so precious in showbiz?

Well, in entertainment, things aren't always as they seem. There are plenty of public figures whose main project on stage or screen is to make you think they're a good person. That's a tricky proposition when it comes to comedy. Personally, I'd much rather people think I might be a bit of a dick and if I come in anywhere under that threshold it feels like a win.

Open virtue and comedy are hard bedfellows to reconcile. As Shakespeare wrote in *Twelfth Night*, 'Dost thou think because thou art virtuous there should be no more cakes and ale?' Conversely, the comedians who take their negative characteristics on stage with them often turn out to be nice people. Do you think Jack Dee is really that grumpy in real life? And come on, deep down you already know how much Romesh loves his kids.

Luckily, there are a small handful of comedians who are exactly what they seem to be and Bob Mortimer would appear to be one of them. A nice man who is able to be extremely funny without being mean to anyone. There are no victims in his jokes.

Do you know how hard that is? It's literally like making an omelette without breaking any eggs.

He has a knack of making you laugh from places you don't expect, like with the following quote: 'At one point I was putting

17 sugars in my tea. I know it's unbelievable and I do wonder sometimes what my mum was thinking to allow it. The weirdest thing was that if I had 18 teaspoons it was too sweet.'

I don't know if that's true or false, or even meant to be a joke, but every time I read it I laugh again.

He'd already had plenty of success throughout his career, but what really tipped Bob into a strong contender for 'Britain's best bloke' was the fishing series he did with Paul Whitehouse. Not only did his usual fundamental decency shine through; we also had two men finding friendship as they recovered from big health scares. Male friendships are hard come by at the best of times, not least in older age, but here we had two of the nation's best-loved comics finding it without resorting to some of the cheaper tropes of an on-screen 'bromance'.

He showed resilience in that series, but Bob appears to have always been that way. His dad died when he was seven and Bob had been a promising footballer until early arthritis curtailed his career. He also supports Middlesbrough, which must have taken more out of him over the years than that triple bypass surgery he had in 2015.

So if it does turn out that Bob ever kicked a homeless person or sold arms to Russia then please keep it yourself. Britain isn't ready to hear it.

HIS BIG DAY

It's a well-worn cliché that from the moment a little girl knows what a wedding day is, she starts planning her own. We never really consider the bloke's version of this. Or if it even exists at all.

Men, ask yourself this question: when was the first time you considered your wedding day and what it might look like? Was it as a little boy? A young man? About five minutes before you were due to say 'I do'?

I always thought I'd get married to a kind and beautiful woman, have children, live in a nice house and enjoy the standard features of what would be deemed to be a happy life. But that was just because I was a general optimist; I never gave much thought to how I'd achieve all that, let alone what colour the place settings would be when the big day came around.

At the point when I (somewhat impulsively) proposed to my wife after just six months (apologies to any bloke whose girlfriend just read this and gave them an impatient glare) I was fully focused on the moment.

My mum, via a family thought process I can't recall the logic of, was the keeper of my nan's engagement ring, which, it had been decreed by the family womenfolk, I'd propose with when that day came. Looking back, I think there was more to it than mere tradition: the hidden agenda was that by being the keeper of the ring, my mum would be in a position to consider my state of mind and whether I was ready or not to make such a big life decision. When it came to it, Emma was so obviously me 'getting out at the top of my game' that my mum almost fumbled the ring as she tossed it to me like an over-zealous fly half.

What I – and many blokes – didn't understand is that a proposal can mean two fundamentally different things to men and women. In my mind, I was asking for her hand in marriage. In hers, it wasn't just that: I was also suggesting a wedding.

Many standard blokes have no idea about the giant process their simple proposal will unleash. They're bidding for the Olympics with no clue as to the kind of the work it will take to stage the event itself.

My family comes from a different socio-economic group to my wife. All I'd known on wedding days were registry offices, beige buffets and men standing around looking generally reluctant. I had no idea someone like me would need to do a tour of stately homes to pick a 'venue'. So I was a bit overwhelmed by it all and didn't play as much of a role as I should have. Emma often used to say, 'You'll turn up on the day and be surprised by your own wedding.' She was right.

On the big day, I was fairly nervous. Like all processes you spend a lot of time imagining yourself into, my wife was able to waltz through the day with great serenity and grace, whereas I – though I enjoyed it – was frequently uncertain as to what was happening next.

The vows were something I'd worried about. I was relieved when they went well, not least because I'd grown up watching *You've Been Framed* and seen far too many grooms pass out at the altar. Why *was* that happening? I'm guessing either nerves or because he and his mates had made the grown-up decision to polish off a bottle of sambuca the previous night.

My wife, having actually given some forethought to the day, looked incredible. I went with the default fashion of the era, which sadly hasn't stood the test of time quite so well. There had been a trend, led by Gazza, of blokes wearing ivory or cream blazers on their wedding day. I had so much gold and ivory on my top half that I looked like the lead in a Bollywood film. The blazer was also very hot, so, like many blokes not used to making a single concession of comfort in favour of fashion, I was frequently overheating – never more so than when my in-laws announced a big surprise.

They'd hired some doves for us to release. It was a lovely gesture but I was a bit rattled, so the handlers patiently showed us how to hold then release the birds. My wife's nestled calmly into her hands (she's always had a way with kids and animals – like Mary Poppins without the parlour tricks). Whereas my dove was a bit cranky from the off and started wriggling around a lot in my hands. The countdown for release was about to begin, so I alerted one of the handlers that I was having problems.

He said, 'Just hold it really tightly. Don't worry, the bird can take a fair bit of pressure.'

So I held the dove as I tight as I reasonably could and . . . it stopped moving. Then the countdown began and I was faced with the prospect that, at the moment we released these two beautiful animals as a transcendent symbol of our love, I was going to lob a dead bird of peace into the air.

As metaphors go, not great.

Luckily, just as the countdown got to one it finally started

THE BRITISH BLOKE DECODED

moving again, though its flight wasn't quite the elegant take-off that my wife's dove managed, and it only seemed to have one good working wing, so went round in manic circles for a while.

Sadly for me, everyone was arranged in a horseshoe around us, so there are photos from every single possible angle of me holding that dove with the face of a man with chronic constipation facing a firing squad.

When it comes to weddings, I might be the last of a generation. As society changes, men will change. A bloke's wedding day is already no longer something he begrudgingly agrees to attend. There may come a time when a young man, having secured that all important 'yes' to a proposal, immediately pulls out brochures from his favourite venues in the area.

Would the average woman want this? Possibly not. There's such a thing as over-correction and I don't care how much society changes – never steal thunder from the bride on her big day.

To prove this point, let me direct you to the TV show *Don't Tell the Bride*. Depending on how seriously you take weddings, this is either the funniest show on telly or a real-life horror film. The idea is that the groom is trusted with the budget and everything from venue selection to food and his bride's dress. I don't know why anyone would enter into this process, but I'm sure a free wedding and some sweet-talking TV producers have something to do with it.

'It'll be fine,' I'm sure they claim, 'We'll keep an eye on him.'

The problem is that if they kept an eye on him and he made sensible decisions, it wouldn't be good telly. So we get a knuckle-headed bloke running around making all sorts of awful decisions, from scrimping on the food to thinking he can get bridesmaids dresses at £15 a pop (why would you anger five women at once?). Some of their decisions cause genuine hurt, but some are bizarre and exemplify that essential boyishness so typical among blokes. One lad planned for the wedding to be at Muscle Beach, Miami. The bride was torn between genuine hurt that some of her family wouldn't be able to attend and the realisation that she was marrying a very strange guy. That wasn't the weirdest it got either. One guy picked the theme of an 'Alien Autopsy'. What kind of weirdo watches documentaries about Roswell and thinks, 'You know what this needs? A disco.'

The reason this nonsense happened is because when the guy popped the question, he wasn't thinking about the day, he was thinking about the union. When offered a central planning role, the bloke within took over and he thought the most important thing was that it was a good laugh.

Traditionally, the decision to propose has either been something blokes haven't given much thought to or have dragged their heels on.

But here's one final thing to consider: since 2010, in the West, the number of women proposing has more than tripled. I guess you could see that as yet another bastion of maleness being chipped away at. However, for many blokes, averse as they are to risk and fuss, taking the job off their hands might well be a blessed relief.

'This tummy is pure muscle.'

Daddy Pig, *Peppa Pig*

MAN-FRUMP

As a working comedian, I was chuffed to be asked on the TV show *Live at the Apollo* for a second time. For most high-profile TV appearances I check my clothing options with my wife, but this time I'd been working away from home and was shopping alone. Mindful of previous catastrophes that have occurred when I've had such scary levels of autonomy, she asked me to send a photo of my outfits hanging up.

The outfits were as follows:

Black polo shirt with white trim.

Black polo shirt with white and brown trim.

Blue polo shirt with yellow trim.

(I hoped that the blue shirt option proved I was willing to be a bit daring; for me, that was the equivalent of Lady Gaga stepping out in a meat dress.)

My wife replied in that enigmatic but loaded way smart women often do. 'I'm sure any of those would be fine, Geoff.'

Looking back, I think that was her subtle way of telling me there was literally no difference. What can I say? I'm good at reading women.

The phenomenon of wives or partners co-piloting their bloke's shopping trips is depressingly common. There are two main reasons for this.

One is that she probably has to attend to make sure the venture even happens in the first place. 'Shopping' is not usually fun for men in the same way it can be for women. It's just an unwelcome occasion where we're subjected to the rank indignity of not doing exactly what we want. There is a small list of exceptions to this – some shopping can be fun, like purchasing PlayStation games or sporting memorabilia – but anything else and I'm trudging around like an eight-year-old boy who got dragged away from a Minecraft party.

Despite my reluctance to undertake shopping trips, I know that on the rare occasions they do happen it's best if my wife is present. She needs to be there to stop me pretending that, yet again, the first shop I went into just happened to have everything I needed. Previously, I've bought trainers by entering a shop, walking in an unbroken line to the pair on the wall I want, then taking them to the counter, barely breaking stride. It's amazing how not fussed you can be when you want to get back to catch the second half. However, it turns out that you have to get granular on this stuff: try them on, walk about in them a bit – forensic stuff like that.

Jeans are another problem. It's taken me years to accept that it's really important to try jeans on, not only standing up but also sitting down. I'm already cursed with the problem of not having an arse, but I exacerbate that further by purchasing jeans where the seat rests somewhere behind my knees. It's a hard enough look to pull off as a rapper, let alone as a forty-six-year-old man getting out of a 2015 SEAT Ibiza.

Over the years, I've wasted enough money and seen enough images of me looking like a mess that even a man-frump like me has taken on board the need to actually try clothes on before buying them. But here's the thing: I'm not going to sacrifice that much leisure time so easily. Consequently, when I have walked around in trainers, sat down in jeans or reached upwards in a new T-shirt and decided I still want them, I look to bulk buy multiple items of the same thing.

I know I'm not alone in bulk buying: it's peak blokery. My whole wardrobe looks like it's set up for identical triplets. In my mind, I justify it by telling myself, 'Steve Jobs only had one outfit, and he invented the iPhone' – as if I'm buying the same Fred Perry shirt six times to free up the mental bandwidth to change global communications forever. It must be an exciting moment for any wife or partner to know exactly what their fella will be wearing for the next five years. You could argue that it loses a bit of excitement and spontaneity, but at least you know what you're getting image-wise. It's like locking in for a five-year fixed-term mortgage. What could be sexier than that?

This uniformity also extends to footwear. For a long time, I only had one pair of shoes and one pair of trainers. The shoes were for work, nights out and weddings, while the trainers took care of literally everything else. I'd describe my process for replacing the trainers as 'reactive'. The criteria usually being whether or not my socks were visible through the soles.

Don't worry, that was the old Geoff. Since then, I've come a long way with footwear. At last count, I had three useable pairs of trainers and two sets of shoes. God knows what would happen if one of my sitcom scripts ever got commissioned by Netflix. I might even consider more than thirty pounds for the next pair.

It's odd how blasé blokes are about their appearance, especially given how much it matters to women. It took me until my late twenties before I began to realise how much notice women took of shoes.

I finally had some sense knocked into me by a Mexican woman I was dating back in the early noughties. She was brilliantly blunt and told me my overall look was that of a *'bolsa de basura para caminar'* ('walking binbag'). She more or less forced me to spend the only bonus I've ever earned entirely on clothes. Her position was: 'I'm not your forever girl, I'm the one who's here to get you ready for when you meet the one who is.'

And she was right. On the night I met my wife, I was wearing some of the newest and most expensive clothes I'd ever bought. I'm not saying that was the only thing which got my wife's attention, but, importantly, my clothes weren't a reason for her to *not* speak to me. In some ways, I sold her a pup because before too long I'd reverted to type and every battle she's waged to improve my image since has been like trench warfare.

There has been perhaps only one occasion when I was on, if not ahead of, the latest fashion trend. In the early noughties, 'man-bags' became a thing. I don't know if it was the fact that blokey icon Joey Tribbiani had one on *Friends*, but I considered them both practical and acceptable. I'd seen my dad's generation stick with briefcases for too long. There was never so tragic a sight as a businessman sitting down on a park bench and pulling out a sad-looking ham sandwich. Briefcases should be for important documents, state secrets – not a flask of tea and some Quavers.

I never understood the resistance to the man-bag and the unspoken implication that it was somehow effeminate. It often came from the same kind of geezers who'd only allow you to drink orange juice in the pub if you were on antibiotics and had a note from the doctor. Even calling it a man-bag is a bit embarrassing. It implies it's full of red meat and bullets. Whereas in reality, it probably contains a Kindle and a set of keys which had started doing damage to your trouser lining.

Maybe the big difference between the average woman and your standard bloke is the fundamentally different ways we view the purpose of clothes – as costume or uniform. The joy many women take in dressing up suggests there are more who tend towards the former. For me, I want my clothes and character to reflect each other: everyday and dependable. The way I look should be an evolution not a revolution. I want the developments in what I wear to proceed at an almost glacial pace, so that, after thousands of years, you'll eventually see the appearance of an upstanding gentleman. Some ladies can wear incredible statement dresses. Some dandy men can look fantastic in a ruffled shirt and velvet suit. Me? I'm not that guy. The way I look is just like I am. It might not be that exciting, but it is something you can rely on.

TABLE FOR ONE

Whether it's Superman and his fortress of Solitude, the Batcave, or even Jesus getting his shit together in the desert, the idea of male solitude is corroborated in popular culture beyond mere stereotype (though I was never sure how realistic Superman's fortress was – if it really was his man cave where was the pool table and jumbo telly?).

During the third lockdown – the long, cold, awful one at the start of 2021 – as a working comic, I'd started to miss life on the road. At the time of the surprisingly benevolent first lockdown of 2020, I'd just come off a long and exhausting work schedule and didn't hanker after gigging as much as I would've thought. Sitting in the garden during that unusually warm spring, I confided to my wife, 'I don't even know if I'll want to go back to touring.'

I can tell you that from the frozen look of intense horror on her face I suddenly realised that the time I spend on the road gigging isn't just for me. It is the one way my wife can get some her-time before bed and watch *Bridgerton* in peace.

However, during that hard lockdown early the following year, I started to seriously miss my former working life. My wife, sensing that frustration, suggested I book into a crap hotel somewhere for a couple of nights to sort my head out. So I did.

Without so much as a reason to be there, I booked into a weird B&B in Newark.

The owners worked out who I was. It must've seemed odd to them that this touring comedian was doing the road bit without the stage bit. I didn't care. Having done this job for so long, I was clearly institutionalised and needed to make tea in a tiny kettle. Even the moment I found myself back on the motorway I started to feel better. Stopping at a roadside Greggs was therapeutic and just being alone in that weird B&B felt restorative. Superman had his giant dome of ice. My fortress of solitude had a dated trouser press.

One of the reasons blokes don't mind a lot of driving is because they recognise the value of that kind of solitude. Modern technology has made being in the car more agreeable, but back in the mid-noughties I'd still happily undertake a long drive armed with nothing more than medium-wave radio. I'd go all the way to Bude and back on a wet Wednesday with no podcasts or audiobooks and only Radio 5 Live for company. I couldn't relate to humans very well but could always tell you the travel news and whether a Labour minister had just resigned. Now, with a whole portfolio of history podcasts to catch up on, driving can be an actual pleasure. I don't know as much about the weather for the week ahead but I do have some excellent trivia on Joseph Stalin.

Personally, I don't mind being alone. Often, I quite like it. I take a perverse joy from staying in budget hotels. There's a Premier Inn in Aberdeen housed in one of the greyest-looking buildings I've ever seen. I think it used to be the head offices for the British School of Motoring. The bleakness seems to compliment and tease out the complex flavours of solitude. I never sleep well in expensive hotels but there's something about the musk of sad businessmen which sets me right at ease.

Is this blokey tendency to seek fortresses, sheds or bleak hotels in the north of Scotland a vestige of our primitive past? I wonder if this is just another remnant of hunting trips. Or the power of those adverts with Lenny Henry.

From time to time, these trips have offered me respite. They have also, sadly, led me to some of the most pathetic moments of my adult life.

I was doing a tour show on the Wirral in the spring of 2022. I was hungover from the previous night in Belfast. I'd had a bit of a 'trains, planes and automobiles' kind of day, so when I finally retired to the suitably plain Travelodge I was thinking only of a snack then sleep.

The vending machine had been vandalised (no doubt when someone realised a Kit Kat cost more than their room). There was nothing else open, so I trudged to my cell knowing that I struggle to sleep when hungry. It was then that I noticed one of the cleaner's carts left in the corridor. Without giving it much thought, I grabbed about sixteen small cartons of UHT milk. My reasoning was that those tiny pots could be enough for a mug of milk before bed. Once in the room – and I can think of no other word for this – I 'decanted' all sixteen of them into the mug, thinking that a milky drink might fill the hole until morning.

You might think that I'd have stopped at four pots and asked what had become of my life, but I kept going.

The moment of clarity came when I went to drink the milk but caught a reflection of myself in the hotel window. There I was, a man in his forties, in a Travelodge on the Wirral drinking a cup of pretend milk he'd patiently decanted. I should've at least done them like vodka shots, to feel like I'd had a night out.

The truth was that life on the road had blurred my perspective on what is normal. Occasional solitude can be good. Too much of it, however, can tempt a man into acts of tragic eccentricity.

And yet, for most blokes I know, the pull of getting away remains. How else do you explain why so many men get into cycling in older age? Fellas who spend all week commuting suddenly start spending their Sundays doing the same, but for fun. They get obsessed with it. It must be weird for their partners when, once again, they appear in the kitchen asking if they're allowed to go out on their bike.

Then there are the runners. I'd imagine one motivation for the middle-aged marathon guys is trying to kid themselves they're still in their 'prime', but a run is also a great time to be alone (though there might be something worrying in how many of these hobbies seem to involve men seeming to flee the place they live).

And what about going for a pint on your own? Is there literally anything more blokey than a man who has decided to do something as sociable as going to a pub, but elected to do it alone? I've done this plenty of times, but now – in another collision of old-world bloke meets new world – I've found that earbuds mean you can even listen to your own music! It's like a portable jukebox in your head.

Let's take it further still. Astronauts are almost exclusively male. Now, more modern, progressive thinkers will tell you that this is down to structural sexism (and it probably is) but I think it's also that some blokes have a deep desire to get as far away from other people as possible. Even if that means going into orbit.

And how about explorers? Christopher Columbus, Sir Francis Drake, Vasco da Gama; people assume they were motivated by the wonder of finding new worlds. Not a chance. They were just looking for some peace and quiet. Sailing to the Americas on the *Santa Maria* was the fifteenth-century of equivalent of 'going down the allotment'.

It's hard to understand the bloke's propensity for solitude. Sure, there's an aspect of retreating from the complications of life, of engineering a situation that is as simple as possible. There's an obvious appeal there. But I also think it could be genetic. Perhaps we're just convinced that we're all splendid chaps and feel honoured to get precious time alone with the best bloke we know – ourselves. Or maybe some of it comes back to some all-important mummy issues . . .

MUMMY ISSUES

'Mums and their sons.' It's a sentence which many girlfriends, wives and sisters will have said ruefully. It's a curious relationship, sometimes oddly close, sometimes damaged and sometimes damaging. Consequently, the relationship between a mother and the principal woman who comes into her son's life can be a delicate thing.

My mum's relationship with my wife started off on a very good footing.

Mum always had a mystical maternal ability to pre-empt things and – in a bizarre moment which I still haven't fully made sense of – I cosmically ordered my wife through her a few months before we actually met in person. Which sounds weird, but let me explain.

In my twenties, I'd been dating for a while and possibly enjoying the bachelor life a bit too much. My mum, sensing my aimlessness, asked me what kind of woman it would take in order for me to settle down.

I described a woman who would turn out to be exactly like my wife.

There were the preferred physical qualities (which you could argue might've been fairly predictable, and favoured by many blokes) – pretty, curvy, etc; however, some were fairly specific:

dark hair, blue eyes and ruby red lips. The personality stuff was where I got really granular, right down to someone who did a bit of charity work in her spare time.

When I met Emma it was like my mum had been involved in some kind of mystical mail-order bride racket.

The first time she met my mum was a key moment. Mum had heard the good reports and was glad my new relationship was going well, but we still needed the royal seal of approval.

It was my sister's wedding day and the house was fizzing with the organised chaos of women doing hair and make-up. Into this stepped Emma. We'd been dating for three months. It was 'serious', so her meeting the family on such an important day was a big deal on top of an already big deal.

Emma said a quick hello, surveyed the military hair and make-up operation going on around her and said, 'Shall I make tea?'

This was just about the best thing you could've said to my mum. She loved tea. I'd say, at a liberal estimate, Mum drank between ten and twelve cups a day. It might explain her energy and focus (or why she had to keep getting up in the night). However, there was one bump in the road ahead. Mum had an odd moral aversion to people having sugar in tea. I have no idea why (it was completely hypocritical as she always had two spoonfuls in coffee). Nevertheless, it was something everyone knew about Jan, so when my wife said, 'Where do you keep the sugar?' there was a moment where time seemed to stand still (imagine the saloon doors swinging, but with blowdryers being turned off and hair straighteners snapping shut).

My mum eventually smiled tightly and said, 'In the cupboard, dear.'

In that moment was a calculation where Mum must've

realised that her son was doing exceptionally well for himself, so she'd have to drop her ideological opposition to sugared tea. However, I'd rarely heard her call women 'dear' before, so this may have been the careful vehicle by which she allowed her irritation to register.

Once we got engaged, my mum – unlike some mums who try to hoard the emotional relationship between mother and son – started disclosing little 'tricks of the trade' to my now fiancée.

'Geoffrey likes a bacon sandwich on a Saturday morning . . . Geoffrey likes having sliced cucumber in the fridge so he can make himself sandwiches.'

I'm sure my soon-to-be wife was inwardly thinking 'Geoffrey can do all those things his fucking self' but she recognised the degree of trust this denoted and duly gestured that she was taking it all in, like shadowing somebody for a day at work.

I was lucky my wife and mother got on. There was a lot of mutual trust and respect (plus my mum was all too aware of some of the utter nightmares I'd dated previously). Even when the mother-wife relationship is going well it can be a tricky one, similar to dads and daughters but with an added layer of intensity.

Societally things have changed a bit, but my mum was not far downstream from a generation that saw sons as a family's best bet to go forth and make big things happen. Maybe they'd make a name for themselves or, in time, once the dad had passed on, be the one who'd step up, and provide for and protect the old dear. That idea had the power to skew the level of investment families would put into boys, not least their mothers.

Consequently, the 'Mummy's little soldier' phenomenon is a

minefield many women around my generation still had to negotiate. There's a lot of upbringing to unpack.

When I was a small boy, the way my mum used to look at me gave a sense of what it must've been like to be born into a dictatorship of succession. My every move was celebrated, my emotions mirrored. I felt like Kim Jong Il, who reportedly had an entourage of sycophants who'd burst into tears whenever he cried.

I was convinced of my own specialness, so you can imagine my dismay when I started attending primary school only to find out that there were *other little soldiers*. Hundreds of them. In fact, the whole world consisted of boys who'd been reared to think they were destined for great things. There couldn't be room for all of us.

There's also a point in the early life of a boy when your mum seems to be a living angel, this loving creature who cares about everything you care about and instinctively seems to know what you need. I'm a fairly hands-on dad, certainly by general historical standards, and my wife isn't excessively mumsy, but if my son falls or cuts himself there's only one person he wants to apply the plaster (and it definitely isn't the one who can't butter toast without ripping the bread to shreds).

In my childhood, many mums still dominated the emotional life of the house, a world in which a boy can almost get swamped by the sphere of a mother's influence. I remember occasional moments when I resented that power.

One of my earliest memories is of being in a shop, and I was cross with Mum for the babyish way she'd spoken about me in company. She asked if I wanted a toy. It was a small, bendable version of the Incredible Hulk. It was a good toy and I really did want it but curtly said, 'No'.

In my mind, I was teaching her some sort of lesson for a grievance I wasn't exactly sure about, but she shrugged, said, 'Fair enough', and put it back on the shelf.

When we got home I went straight to my room, shut the door, lay on the bed and cried my eyes out. I guess it was my first act of true rebellion against the sometimes suffocating regime of maternal love, but sadly it was a very shit form of rebellion as all that happened was I missed out on a really cool toy.

We speak a lot about male power in the public domain, but I've often thought about how the female power which often presides in the home and private sphere can be equally compelling on a day-to-day basis. Mums can control a child's narrative, certainly if they're with them all day and if Daddy doesn't come home from work until early evening. They can fashion their sons to hold almost any opinion with anything from light suggestion to full-on politburo-style propaganda.

There's a point in the early part of any small child's life where the mother and child are so intuitively connected that they almost become a separate unit in the house. I remember when my son was young and I was particularly busy I'd experience this. My wife and son had developed little catchphrases about my behaviour. 'Silly daddy!' my wife might say and he'd echo back 'Silly daddy!', and I'd be thinking, 'Hang about. Have I become a sitcom character in my own life?'

I felt compelled to justify my place in the hierarchy of the house.

'Silly daddy, is it? Who a few years back got us on a different mortgage which allowed us to ride out the chaotic reign of Kwasi

Kwarteng without having to worry. I'm VAT-registered mate, what have you ever done? Plus, I've been on *Mock the Week* . . . No, they didn't ask me back . . . touché my friend, *touché*.'

Why wouldn't a boy be in thrall to his mother during early life? She's loving, kind and responds to any new knowledge he's acquired like he might be in contention for a Nobel Prize.

I love my son more than life itself. Also, as a fellow boy, he makes sense to me. He looks very similar to me, has similar personality traits, he even shapes some of his handwriting the same way I do and has the exact same competence when it comes to looking for something in a cupboard (none). Genetically, it feels like a linear progression.

But, however close I am to my son, or fathers are to their daughters, we didn't carry them. Mothers of sons not only have the tactile legacy of having carried them but also the curious reality that, out of their female body, they produced a male. They now have a chance to make a man, to sculpt him, direct him and improve on some of the useless gits they've had to endure.

Many blokes from my generation were among the last to be indulged by their mothers on such a fundamental level and when I visit parks with my son today, I see how much things have changed. Mothers coax their daughters to be braver on the apparatus, bolder with their bodies and with risk. Why wouldn't they? They've seen Katniss Everdeen kick arse in the *Hunger Games*; they've seen Rey fly the *Millennium Falcon* in *Star Wars* and Liz Truss run the country (maybe scratch that last one).

However, there are still fundamentals involved in raising a

boy which change how you relate to them. Young boys on average use fewer words on a less frequent basis than their female counterparts. Whatever feminist beliefs a mother takes into parenting a boy, they'll be confronted by the reality that – certainly between the ages of three and six – he will just seem a bit less *capable* than females of the same age. Consequently, the mum might give him a bit more support, a bit more praise, a bit more encouragement, and lo, during the boy's most formative period, what he remembers is getting a lot of credit for doing the bare minimum (medal, anyone?).

I wonder if this helps explain the roots of mansplaining. When a small boy has successfully taken on information and relayed it to his mother she can act delighted, so his takeaway might be that all women need simple things explained to them.

I saw this phenomenon recently at a mate's house. The kid came back from preschool and said, 'Mummy, once upon a time there were dinosaurs!'

Delighted that he'd finally retained a single piece of information from his day, the boy's mother trilled, '*Dinosaurs*?? Tell me more about these dinosaurs!'

I wonder if the kid was then thinking, 'Hang about, love . . . you're a fully grown woman, shouldn't you know about that kind of stuff?'

Meanwhile, my mate, his dad, was looking over and competitively announced, 'A lot of people think the T-Rex was around during the Jurassic era but it didn't actually emerge until the Cretaceous.' He then smugly went back to staring at the telly.

In the space of a minute, the young boy's mum had thrown a ticker-tape parade for fuck all and his dad had reminded him who the true household expert was. Put that same boy in the boardroom forty years later and there might be a part of him trying to shout louder than the other males and expecting acclaim for repeating a woman's idea back to her.

It creates a challenge for the rest of the bloke's life that his first experience of a female loving him is complete and unconditional. Because in the real world, attracting and retaining a woman's love is highly conditional: it must be cultivated and earned on a daily basis. As it should be. If, like me, you married well and at the end of each week she's still willing to let you sleep in the same bedroom, you're doing alright.

Another challenge for blokes is how you evolve your relationship with your mother as you age; how does someone who was so physically and emotionally bound to you in your infancy become a friend in adult life? I've known many men who hit a point where they suddenly found their devoted mums, the level of their attention, the vivid scrutiny of their love, becoming oppressive.

One of the successful things my mum did, once she clocked that I was starting to file her away into the 'mumsy' role, was to change the relationship. She started debating with me about politics and challenging my reasoning. As a result, I wasn't able to pigeonhole her quite so easily. However, one thing she could never stop doing was – on the occasions I'd visit – sitting and watching me eat. Even when I was a man in my early thirties, she loved to watch me stuff my face. I found it odd. Eating isn't a performing art. But I indulged it as best I could because I understood that it was different for her.

When your body once fed a little thing within it, sharing all the same nutrients and energy that you were taking in, and when that creature spent the early bit of its life seeming like a hopeless little ball of chaos, it must be hard later on to maintain anything like a normal relationship.

BLOKEY FILM REVISIONS #3:
DIRTY DANCING

I don't mind admitting I was bang into this film as a kid. My sister watched it once a day every day for a whole summer. I had the luxury of grumbling performatively, but only for the benefit of the other lads present. I was totally caught up not just in the story and music, but in the classy-looking world of America in 1963.

Luckily for me, my wife is also a *Dirty Dancing* devotee. A few years ago, Secret Cinema put on a *Dirty Dancing* experience. Once again, I was able to play the reluctant male, being dragged along to something I had no interest in. Full disclosure: I was carrying watermelons with the best of them (apologies to any true blokes who do not get this reference . . . or at least pretend not to).

The premise of the film is fairly straightforward, sitting as it does somewhere between *Lady Chatterley's Lover* and *Romeo and Juliet*. The cosseted middle-class girl is swept off her feet by a diamond in the rough (in this case a dancer called Johnny) who is going to show her 'another' side of live (in these kind of stories, 'another side of life' often means 'powerful orgasms').

The dad starts off from a different place to Mr Banks in Mary Poppins. His daughter is the apple of his eye and says 'daddy' in that way in which American girls evolved their speech patterns to absolutely ensure they get a pony. But over the course of the film, as 'Baby' starts delving into the steamy underworld of the dancers working at the Catskills resort, a wedge is placed between father and daughter. Bit by bit, the upstanding Dr Jake Houseman is fibbed to by Baby and the whole thing comes crashing down when he has to patch up a potentially lethal backstreet abortion on Johnny's ex-squeeze, Penny. Baby had been LYING to her daddy (hand that pony back immediately). Dr Houseman is furious with his daughter. We, the manipulated audience, dutifully sit there thinking, 'Don't be so harsh, let Baby be free to live her life . . .!'

But you know what? As I sat in the Secret Cinema field re-watching this film with an army of women, once again completely buying into it, I started to think, 'Hang on just a *minute*. This is America in the early sixties. This hard-working father has taken his family on holiday in the Catskills resort. He knows it won't be long before she's a full-grown woman who buggers off to join the Peace Corps or whatever costly endeavour middle-class kids wasted their time with back then. He simply wants to spend some quality time with his daughter.'

What father wouldn't have issues with this 'Johnny Castle' prick? The flashy name alone should strike fear into the heart of any self-respecting patriarch. Tell me a conscientious dad who wouldn't be struck with terror by his daughter fooling around with some leather-jacket-wearing prima donna called 'Johnny Castle'. Or Johnny anything for that matter. Now, he may not have been the one who got Penny pregnant, but in early 1960s America, the combination of the name 'Johnny' and that much Brylcreem was likely to get a girl knocked up at a distance of fifty feet.

And let's not completely exonerate Baby from all this. She lies to her dad and gets needlessly drawn into other people's dramas. Whether or not the dad does go into a massive man-sulk, he saves a young woman's life (let's give credit to the film for indirectly making a pro-choice point without ramming it down anybody's throat).

By the end of the film, however, we've become transfixed by other things.

'He did the lift! Johnny did the lift!'

But what about the character who literally stopped a young woman dying? How can we be so manipulated that we rank 'the lift' above the preservation of life (though I concede it was an *amazing* lift)? But no, poor old Dr Jake Houseman is the grumpy old coot who needs to shape up, get with the times and let his daughter do whatever the hell she wants.

Despite my blokey re-reading, the emotional climax of the film still retains a fair bit of power.

It's the final dance and a glum-faced Baby is sitting with her parents. Old Johnny 'snake hips' Castle comes bowling over to the old man and utters the immortal line, 'Nobody puts Baby in a corner.'

The women at the Secret Cinema showing all cheered at this line, but I wondered how many of them had kids now. And of the ones who did, I wondered how many would be left with any respect for their husband if some flash git strode over and mugged him off in front of his wife and daughter.

At that point I wished Dr Jake Houseman had stood up and said, '*You know what, mate? Maybe Baby is getting older and maybe it is no longer my right to tell her exactly what to do with her life, but I have raised her. No doubt old muggins here will be paying for her personal growth when she's pissing about in the Peace Corps.*

'So what's YOUR plan, Johnny Castle? Everyone knows dancing isn't exactly a young man's game. What are you gonna do when you've paso dobled so hard your hips blow out at the age of thirty-six?

'I did not work my arse off in medical school to put my daughter through college just so she could bank-roll some chancer – who, let's not forget, five minutes ago was turning tricks for bored housewives.

'So maybe nobody should "put" Baby in a corner, but I'd argue given the years and money I've invested in my daughter, if anyone should even consider putting Baby in a corner, it'd probably be me . . . or my wife. Sorry, dear.'

Of course I didn't say any of this, and I was up at the end having a dance to 'Time of My Life' with the girls.

But if we're imagining realistic sequels for these films, we all know that Baby would've hit her late twenties and suddenly developed a taste for men with qualifications and pensions. And in that film, Johnny Castle is a lot of things, but he's not your average bloke. For that look no further than the calm and dependable Dr Jake Houseman.

I'D RATHER DIE THAN GO ON A SPA DAY

'Pampering' is a common leisure pursuit for women. The simple act of being a lady is so iconic that it sometimes necessitates paid minions to file away at their nails or give those eyebrows a little massage. Just mention the words 'spa day' and see the mystical quality of those two words play out on the face of the woman you're with, in the same way blokes react when you suggest a 'Leo Sayer' (all-dayer).

Most blokes don't have spa day at the top of their list of leisure pursuits. We do reward ourselves, but those rewards rarely result in feeling and looking better. For example, one of my favourite things to do is spend a whole day at the cricket. If you caught me staggering back to the Premier Inn around 11pm after a day at the Test match you wouldn't see someone looking rejuvenated. The only 'face peel' I'd be sporting is my own skin because I'd reverted to not wearing sun cream.

For me, pampering has never felt enjoyable, to the point my wife has stopped suggesting spa days. She's able to submit to the full cucumber on the eyes indulgence of the affair, whereas I would dread the experience from the moment it was booked.

Right from arrival I'm expected to do things I find highly unnatural. First, you get given the biggest dressing gown you've ever seen, roughly three stories high as it's handed, folded, across the reception desk. Then you get the complimentary slippers. I think this is all part of the ritual; the ridiculously springy towelling of the robe represents a transition from people's scratchy everyday reality. And when else do you wear freshly laundered slippers, or taste water with so much mint and lemon?

On my first visit to a spa day, I presumed I'd get changed and head straight to the treatment room.

No. I was expected to come back and sit in reception, dressed in this ridiculous manner. In public, with the draught dancing around my partially exposed balls, my chest hair on show and the gown occasionally flapping open (because, being a cack-handed man, I couldn't tie it properly).

You do, however, see the occasional experienced male spa user who knows what he's doing. He sits in reception reading a broadsheet newspaper with breathtaking conviction. You try to follow his lead, maybe sip a glass of the weird water, but feel like you're impersonating a millionaire waiting for an X-ray.

Men from the continent seem a lot more at ease with the whole spa day experience. Massages instinctively feel a bit more European. Plus it's an extra challenge for British blokes to relax in fluffy slippers, given that those slippers rarely come with socks.

Then there's the issue of how bloody long the thing lasts. Even thirty minutes for a massage is a long time to be lying face down with your face through that weird hole. It feels like you're in a submission position. What kind of psycho can take an hour of that? What kind of vestiges of former imperial privilege reside that you can casually allow a stranger to attend to your comfort for that long? I reckon they're the kind of people who'd think nothing of being fanned by a giant palm leaf.

Maybe women can do it because they've had altitude training

173

in the form of long hairdressing appointments. I've had wrist surgery concluded more promptly than it takes my wife to have a cut and colour.

I'm not saying all women enjoy their hair appointments taking longer than a Test match; they don't. My wife has to psyche herself up for one, whereas, for me, going to get my haircut is often a snap decision, the by-product of happening to see a barbers while out and noticing that my hair is starting to create the silhouette of a motorcycle helmet.

Massages also carry the angsty concern over whether or not you get an erection. Being more overtly sexually driven creatures, a lot of men will worry that they might embarrass themselves by getting a boner. It's very difficult to dissociate from the fact that massage is something you normally do during sexy times with your partner.

Nervous erections are a real phenomenon and especially galling once you hit middle age, when such shows of potency are generally harder to come by, but here they are showing up like family dropping by without prior notice. Thankfully, I've never had this situation occur, but the risk of it keeps me on my toes and makes it very hard to fully submit to the experience.

When the masseuse says, 'How's the pressure?' I'm half tempted to say, 'Well, I nearly had a panic attack a minute ago but I think I'm finally starting to chill out.'

My wife and I will often reunite having had simultaneous treatments. She's in a dreamy state and ready to go back to the hotel room for a blissful nap on those high-thread-count sheets. I, meanwhile, head to the bar for a pint to steady the nerves.

In the same way pubs and bookies have made those environments more inviting to women over the last twenty years, my proposal is that we should look at making spa days more enticing to blokes. For us, it's all about distractions. I'm not saying massage rooms should automatically have sport on, but it should at least be an option. Also, if I'm right and spa days do make most blokes nervous, how about offering a relaxing beer beforehand? Next to the mint and lemon water they could have a discreet tap dispensing Moretti.

And we need to stop with the giant fluffy robes. We should be allowed to enter the spa in our own shorts and T-shirts – and yes, I recognise that replica football shirts should not be allowed. This is a classy establishment after all.

I'm not an animal.

DADDY'S SPECIAL SPAG BOL

*Eight per cent of UK men only cook from
scratch once a month.*

Recently, my wife and son were away for the night, so I was keen
to take advantage of having the house to myself. The clichéd idea
of how blokes respond to such freedom would run along the lines
of walking around naked and drinking whisky on the treadmill.
In reality, it's never really like that when you're the adult version
of home alone.

The main thing to exploit is the novelty of being in your own
house with the freedom to decide what's for dinner (and watch
cricket without a collective groan). So I decided to cook myself a
nice meal. Steak with thick-cut chips. Not only that, I preceded
it with a crude but enjoyable prawn cocktail starter. I'd also been
to the Co-op to get a nice bottle of red wine. At this point, it
occurred to me: I was essentially on a date with myself. My wife,
given a night at home on her own would never do the same. I was
acting like a bloke in the first six months of a new relationship
with a woman. Yet here I was, forty-six years into a love affair
with myself and clearly that love was burning brighter than ever
(plus, I was pretty sure I was going to get lucky that night).

Canvassing the opinion of other blokes, it seems my response
to being home alone is fairly common, but I can't think of a single
woman in a long-term relationship who would do the same.
Indeed, before we had kids, when I was on the road most nights

doing gigs, I'd implore my wife to make herself a decent evening meal but would usually return home to find yet another bowl and solitary spoon by the sink. Instead of wowing herself in the kitchen, she'd had Weetabix for dinner.

If you throw in the fact that men seem to be happier with their own solitude, you might start to wonder whether blokes are just more *into* themselves (I can already feel the female readers going 'Duh?').

It wouldn't be out of character – you are, after all, talking to mummy's little soldier here. If I'm honest, the little boy in me still believes I should be allowed to do what I want most of the time. I can be bang in the middle of bringing the shopping into the house and my wife will find me sitting looking at my phone. The more evolved part of my brain recognises that this isn't a reasonable whim, but from time to time, that part of me absents itself while the other bit looks up retro clips of nineties football despite the fact that there are still Co-op bags sitting outside the front door.

Cooking seems to sit differently in the minds of most women I know. My mum, wife and sister (the holy trinity of my female universe) all reported that making dinner itself could be a chore but that having to *think* of what the meal should be was the most draining part. Because blokes generally cook less often, our contributions can acquire the short-term razzamatazz of a showbiz cameo. We're very good at talking up our stint in the kitchen. When have you heard a woman burst into a front room and proudly announce: 'Hey everybody! Tonight I'm doing my special spag bol!' and stand there with arms outstretched like they just bought everyone in the pub a drink (and btw – 'special spag bol' just means we'll use stock and basil).

The truth is we've changed a lot and many modern blokes love cooking. Or rather, modern blokes love *cheffing*. My little boy learned from an early age that if he fancied something quick and simple he'd ask his mum to knock him up eggs on toast, but if he wanted something fancy she had to step aside while dad went into full-on Gordon Ramsay mode.

I live for when my wife asks if I fancy cooking this weekend. If it was the other way round she would simply have a quick look in the fridge, sniff a couple of things to check whether they were edible then turn out a lovely pasta dish ten minutes later. But that's too easy. I prefer the two-hour browse of the internet to find something needlessly exotic.

In this situation, most blokes will then proceed to make a lot of mess as they strive for the showstopper of the family's weekly diet. Often the things we cook won't even be suitable for the kids we're supposed to be feeding, then we'll sit sulking as, for some bloody reason, the four-year-old didn't want to try our spicy Thai noodles.

My own noodle recipe, like so many of the meals blokes tend to favour cooking, can all be done in one dish. I have mates who are excellent amateur chefs, but they still favour one-pot solutions. There's a gender divide not just in what we cook but in how we cook it. I don't know many men who are good at doing roast dinners. Roasts seem to require that mystical female skill of multitasking and an even bigger multitude of pots and pans. The difficulties men have doing roasts could even be seen to reflect our issues in and around foreplay. A roast requires forethought; you have to get the oven warm before you start and even then, to do the thing *properly*, it'll probably take a minimum of an hour. This is why many blokes favour the wok. Get it hot really quickly, chuck in the meat and it's all done in seven minutes. Sound familiar?

If roasts skew female, the barbecue has become almost comically aligned with blokery. There's something primal about cooking outside (granted, cavemen probably didn't make a herb-infused marinade and slice up halloumi, but still). Searing meat outside also calls to the ancient hunter-gatherer brain. The fact that I 'gathered' the meat from Sainsbury's doesn't matter. Some women think blokes like barbecuing for the love of food. But, like most things, it's just another excuse to be alone for a bit. You also know that any men who do talk to you will have to talk exclusively about meat, which is generally safe territory.

If you don't have time to destroy the kitchen or smoke out half the neighbourhood, the act of ordering takeaway is also replete with blokey rituals. When I was single, ordering a takeaway was a simple affair. Whatever the menu, I simply chose the dishes with the most chilli symbols next to them, asked for extra chilli sauce and added some rice. That took two minutes, the phone call was thirty seconds, and half an hour later I was burning my tongue in front of the football. Simple.

Once you're in a relationship, you have a very specific job when it comes to takeaways. Namely, that you have to order it, because for some reason when it comes to calling an Indian restaurant, your wife will suddenly turn into a 1950s housewife who's incapable of speaking to another person without your guiding hand.

If you're an elite bloke, you'll also drive to the restaurant to get that crucial 10 per cent discount. And once there, you have to make small talk and agree to buy a beer at the bar that costs the same amount as the 10 per cent discount.

In a way, it's odd that food ever strayed outside the realms of the blokey jurisdiction. When it comes to 'protect and provide', no one said you couldn't 'provide' a lovely meal (even if it does have way too much salt, chilli and you may never get the smell out of the kitchen).

YOU'VE GOT A SISTER?

Forty-one per cent of British men say they have friends they 'like but don't bother to see'

One broad criticism of blokes is that the scale and quality of our friendships diminishes as we age. In our late teens and early twenties, we exist in literal tribes of man pals, but that rapidly falls off a cliff somewhere around the age of twenty-six and by the end you're down to a couple of legacy mates and that husband of the woman your wife recently befriended (who you have nothing in common with and who talks too much about Formula 1). It's all the more galling when women still seem to be recruiting friends at this time in life: friends from NCT, mums from school, someone they spoke to once at Morrisons . . . Whereas your friendship portfolio is like print media: in a constant state of managed decline.

The lazy blame for this phenomenon is often put down to a long-term partnership with a woman. She will – apparently – survey your friendship group like an incoming football manager and conduct a selective cull where many muckers end up on the transfer list. Despite being a cliché, this does happen a fair bit. Indeed, her assessment that some of your friends are 'wrong 'uns' is often proved to be objectively true (sometimes in a court of law). More often than not, however, the dwindling number of mates is entirely the bloke's fault.

Blokes should invoke one of their own core values and take

some bloody responsibility for this sad state of decline. Most men don't make the effort. We don't ask what's really going on in each other's lives. We don't remember each other's birthdays. In fact, to do so might create suspicion and resentment within the group, as you're just creating work for everyone else.

Like all things which seem inexplicable, there's a solid reason why most men act like this, however unsatisfactory it may be. The more you know about people the more you care and worry about them. The blokey psyche can drive a lifelong attempt to divest itself of such complicated responsibilities wherever possible. There's a liberating element in not having too many attachments. It's lonely, but, on the plus side, Christmas shopping can all be done in a lunch break.

The British bloke has a further barrier in that we're not so hot on tactility with each other. I've noticed the difference when I go abroad. In many Mediterranean countries, the man-hugs are full frontal. In the Middle East, men will often give each other a friendly kiss with no trace of self-consciousness. Meanwhile, in Britain, we rely on the handshake, which allows our torso to be as far away from the other man's as possible at the point of contact. There are hugs, but these often manifest in the form of two forearms sort of locked in front of each other and a manly slap on the back, which could be seen as camaraderie but usually means 'OK, I think that's more than enough!'

There's a brilliant film called *Up in the Air* starring George Clooney, which engages with this theme of men favouring a simple life. The main character is a travelling corporate trouble-shooter who goes into struggling companies and fires staff on the management's behalf. His USP – and the thing he's paid to do motivational talks for – is that he keeps everything in one rucksack. He has no partner and no children, he just roams from one place to the next, has meaningless hook-ups and a swim in the hotel pool, and then moves on to the next corporate cull. Eventually he desires connections but I'd be lying if I didn't admit that during the first act of the film I was thinking, 'This guy's got it made!'

His life is grey and limited, but it's peaceful. Plus he seems to be having a laugh.

I think a lot of women occasionally wonder if blokes' lives are generally more of a laugh. On a surface level, I think they might be. I used to have a comedy routine which I'd end by saying, 'Then I leave for work; two miles down the road, I've forgotten I've got a family.'

Obviously that's not true but there's a noticeable difference in mine and my wife's capacity to just 'switch off' from family stuff.

This detachment from the details of life can have a downside. You could be twenty-six years into a friendship with one of your best pals and find yourself saying something like, 'You've got a sister?' Blokes simply don't spend enough time asking each other what's going on in their lives.

Why is that? Maybe there's a desire not to seem impertinent or – worse still – nosey. We also recognise that grown-up blokedom involves a lot of stress and responsibility, so the last thing you want to do on an all-dayer is get deep and meaningful. You want to talk bollocks, not have Big Steve tilt his head sympathetically and say something like, 'But Geoff, how did losing at darts make you feel? Like, *really* feel.'

Talking bollocks can be dismissed as completely meaningless but it's not – there's a code there, if you wish to decipher it.

The bloke telling you he can't watch the Premiership any more because of all the diving is telling you he doesn't like change.

The guy who thinks the Bond franchise has lost its way is . . . also telling you he doesn't like change (look, once you reach a certain age, a lot of it is about the fear of change).

I also wonder if that mate in your friendship group who's started constantly wanging on about social justice issues just wants it acknowledged that he's a nice guy. We could save hundreds of minutes of virtue signalling if we just put an arm around him early doors and said, 'You, Jakey boy, are a quality human being. Now can we shut up about Greta and get back to talking bollocks?'

One thing which has been a game changer for bloke's friendships – and indeed all human interactions – is the advent of WhatsApp groups. Technology has finally found a way of keeping groups of men in regular touch with each other. These groups can be a laugh, a distraction and – sometimes – a comfort. They're so useful to male camaraderie that if we'd had them during the First World War I doubt any shots would've been fired or poetry written.

There are pranks too, lots of them. One of which came to public prominence in early 2023 when a group of blokes managed to get a stunt onto a live *Match of the Day*, with planning so intricate it was like *Ocean's Eleven* on a stag-do.

The sting was this: what initially seemed like an interesting viral video that most blokes would watch (like a honey badger fighting a lion) would, right at the last minute, ambush you with the high pitch soundtrack from a porn film of a woman reaching a noisy climax. The pranksters had somehow changed one of the crew's ringtone to that sound, and rang it repeatedly.

Gary Lineker reacted with reasonable good grace as the noise sounded off time after time in the *MOTD* commentary booth. Loads of blokes were laughing in recognition, but those watching with their other half might have quickly had to explain why a pornographic sound effect had them laughing in fond familiarity.

Bringing another bloke down a peg or two is an intrinsic part of who we are. Admittedly it's unfortunate that we don't communicate enough in the first place and that when we do it can be in the sound of humiliating sex noises. This does begin to change in middle age. There's something about the softening effect of fatherhood and losing your own parents that has tuned me and my mates into each other's real lives a bit more. We show more concern about the big life events. Thankfully, it seems that when actual life takes us down a peg or two we're there to raise each other back up. However, on a day-to-day basis we still don't delve too deeply into what's going on with one another. When blokes don't ask their mates the real questions it's often because they perceive it as 'bother' and they personally have a general desire not to be bothered.

Talking about the big things is an effort, but the problem is that over time, those minutes when you're not disclosing the real issues stack up. They become hours, days and months when you're not downloading your deepest fears and resentments to anyone. If you're not engaged in talking therapies either, this can eventually manifest in destructive behaviours.

It's hard for many blokes to be a good friend. My wife often has to coach me. She, like many women, is bewildered when I return from two days away with the lads without a single new piece of information about them or their families.

The exchange normally follows this pattern:

Her: So, how are the boys?
Me: Good.
<Beat>
Her: What's been happening?
Me: [worried] What have you heard?
Her: I mean in their lives. I know Austin's youngest has started
*   college and hasn't Mandy got a new job?*
Me: Er, I don't know about any of that.
Her: You didn't ask any of your friends about what is going on
*   in their lives? That's a bit sad.*
Me: Eh? That's what was great about it. We spent forty-eight
*   hours together and barely scratched a millimetre beneath*
*   the surface. It's practically a superpower!*

So we need to evolve a bit, but that's not to say that men suddenly have to transform themselves into full-on head-tilting empaths who, instead of talking about the upcoming Ashes series, are asking whether you've ever felt 'genuine intimacy' during sex. It's just a case of checking in and keeping up with the main developments in each other's lives. The last thing you want to do is to be comforting your mate over the breakdown of his third marriage when you're not even fully sure what happened to the second.

'ER INDOORS

Women file for 62 per cent of all divorces in England and Wales.

I realise that with a chapter heading like 'Er Indoors, I might be running the risk of losing a certain kind of reader (unlike 'the Mrs', ''Er Indoors' is very much a phrase that now sits squarely in the past). I guess what I really wanted was your attention because this chapter is actually about something painfully underdiscussed: men's difficulty in talking about the state of their relationship.

In my long career of observing the average bloke in his natural habitat, there seems to be a real issue with talking about such problems. I'm not saying I actively want to hear my pals complain about their wives or girlfriends, but it's peculiar how rarely I've heard any man make specific criticism of his other half in my company.

For context, it should be said that me and my friends have all done pretty well for ourselves, and a group of men so clearly punching above their weight will always be mindful of not rocking the boat. When we get together it looks like a reunion for a group of people who met on series three of *Love Is Blind*.

One reason that men complain less about their relationships – and marriage in particular – is there's plenty of evidence that married life provides men with more benefits than it does women. Life expectancy for women goes down a whole year when they are

THE BRITISH BLOKE DECODED

married (maybe the toilet seat being up really is an existential risk). And being divorced carries such an additional premium of male risk that the phrase 'happy wife, happy life' starts to sound like something your doctor should write on a prescription. After their female partner dies, men are in more danger of dying, and over a longer period, than a woman is, should the man be the first to go.

When blokes of my dad's generation lost their wives there was a clear gender difference in how they dealt with it, possibly exacerbated by the degree to which men of that era depended on their partners. If she did go first, the poor bastard wouldn't know what to do with himself. Within a week, he'd be eating dog food in the dark or trying to wash his Y-fronts in the shower. It's a bit different the other way around. If the bloke goes first the woman will of course be sad, but that's less likely to stop her going on a world cruise with her best mate.

However, this data doesn't let us know exactly how happy men are within those marriages. Any creature who eats and sleeps better will live longer, but that doesn't mean their relationship is necessarily happier or more romantically fulfilling. Remember, animals in captivity live longer (and if my wife is reading I'd like to be clear that I am no way comparing myself to one of the rhinos at Woburn).

Could it possibly be that women are simply better to be around? If I stop and think of the older couples I know, I don't see much of a difference in terms of general likeability. For every grumpy old git there's a battle-axe. For every inattentive man there's a woman who exits social gatherings early because she's 'got one of her headaches coming on'.

Blokes generally don't complain about their relationships as much as women, but they can sometimes act in a way which suggests they're angry about *something*. In that survey, which revealed that one of men's top gripes with women is that they rarely initiate sex, it emerges that another big bugbear is that women rarely say sorry when they're in the wrong. I wonder if this is a resentment which grows after couples have children. Partly because the bloke no longer feels comfortable seeking apologies, as his status in the house has irrevocably changed and he needs to 'fall back' a bit.

This is natural, as dropping down a level helps to provide a steady backdrop to prioritise the needs of an infant. Blokes don't generally mind, either; they're just grateful she seems to know how to keep this tiny thing alive. What this new household ranking does is encourage men to drop a lot of issues for a quiet life. In short, blokes start to lose a lot of arguments they could have won. This isn't necessarily a problem – more a strategic retreat, which can last several years. Or for the rest of their lives.

Some blokes allow this to breed resentment and end up acting out in destructive ways which ultimately hurt them too. They lost too many arguments, said sorry too many times when they thought they were in the right, and got rejected sexually so many times that their stupid penis found them in bed with Claire from accounts (I've no idea why these examples always include someone from 'accounts' – particularly odd given that people working in this department have rarely struck me as sexual titans).

It's a dumb kind of self-destructive retribution that blokes seem to specialise in, an elevated version of punching the wall to show they're angry, then spending the next twelve hours in A&E.

The problem is, a lot of us don't really know how we expected a marriage to feel, in the same way we never think about our wedding day when proposing marriage. Blokes never had romantic fairy tales to dream about as small boys. The TV and films we watch rarely contain specific ideas on how women should act in relation to us once we're in a relationship.

Our culture may heavily implant in us ideas of how woman should look, but even then the average bloke remains fairly easily pleased. Similar to their views on body shape, most blokes are fairly open-minded about behaviour too. Women aren't expected to be gallant or romantic or funny, just . . . nice.

If men do have gripes about women's behaviour, it'll normally come down to general issues with mood across a longer period of time. Even then it'll take a while before he'll feel able to mention the atmosphere at home to any of his friends, and it still might take the form of a classic piece of understatement like 'she had a face on'.

The more progressive reader might baulk at old-fashioned language like that, but not all the old phrases are without merit – if someone says their Mrs 'had a face on' it can be understood to have been one of those days when she was on the warpath and the little annoying things he did which usually got a free pass would face the scrutiny of the Chilcot Inquiry.

I've also got no doubt that the stereotypical bloke has his own equivalent of 'waking up with a face on' – such as if his first three answers of the day are delivered in the form of a grunt. Or if his solution to a problem sounds suspiciously like the exact same one his wife suggested several minutes ago when he wasn't listening.

In the event that men are profoundly unhappy at how their relationships are going, the language and opportunity for them to express this dissatisfaction is limited. Compare this to the discourse on a show like *Loose Women*. The whole concept of this highly successful programme is that it's socially acceptable – encouraged, even – for women to get together and bond through sharing, which can include criticism of either how rubbish their bloke is or blokes are in general. The show works because it's a phenomenon we recognise, plus we understand it to be a legitimate form of female bonding. This is in serious contrast to how most blokes operate when it comes to criticising their partner.

Moaning about your wife – certainly in the male friendship groups I've been part of – would seem a bit off at best and, at worst, a bit treacherous. Not only that, you're also burdening your mates with information they'll have to pretend they don't know about next time they see her. If anything, the men I know tend to eulogise about their wives to the group: 'She's great with the kids', 'I don't know where she finds the energy', 'I think she only married me for a bet' – that sort of thing. It's a far cry from older generations of men who would happily cast their wives as screeching harridans whose only goal in life was to piss on their joy.

Women, on the other hand, seem to have little problem sharing intimate details about their bloke, even if it undermines him in the eyes of their female friends.

My wife is fairly respectful in this regard, but I've no doubt that during past relationships I've shared a meal with women who've previously had intimate details about me relayed to them over a glass of wine. I'm pretty sure I've spoken to women who've seen a detailed impression of my 'sex face'.

Maybe blokes don't do the same because moaning about our

situation threatens the crucial idea that we've done well for ourselves, that we married above our level and are 'punching'. The man who does routinely moan about his wife is viewed with deep suspicion by the group. What does he want us to say in return? To *collude*? To criticise *his* wife? There's always the risk that he's just having an off day and the next time you see him you're now the guy who criticised the love of his life.

And how the hell are you supposed to make eye contact with his Mrs next time you see her once you're in possession of private information? Like how you know she got drunk on their only romantic date night of the year and passed out in an empty bath.

It may sound old-fashioned, but a lot of blokes feel that stuff like that is better remaining between couples. Possibly because we know full well that in the grand scheme of embarrassing behaviours which could be shared we'd probably come out worse. It's a form of wishful thinking, that if we adopt some kind of mafia-style 'omerta' it may be honoured in return – and the fact that we left the family's passports on the Heathrow Express might get brushed under the carpet.

There is, consequently, a bit of a gulf in the capacity blokes have to communicate the overall health of their relationship. This can lead to men not being able to pull the trigger on situations they haven't been happy in for a long time, as a lack of general discussion about what's going on in their love life can allow them to live in a state of denial. All of which leaves blokes at a significant disadvantage in terms of how they process the way their love lives are going.

I'm not saying that women don't stay in bad marriages – or indeed feel that they literally can't leave – but rather that duty can be a disproportionately high reason men don't feel like they *should* leave and why they remain in loveless situations even when this doesn't benefit them, their wife or their kids.

Women seem to be significantly better at valuing their own happiness, eventually. And men who do pursue happiness are often mistaking that for a younger woman who gives them the kind of erections they haven't had since the late nineties.

So the simple answer would seem to be this: let's talk more. Let's moan more. Let's gossip more. Let's do those unflattering impressions of our other halves which makes our friends squeal with laughter during whatever the male equivalent is of a bottomless brunch.

However, there's still a problem.

There's a very good reason no TV exec has ever commissioned a regular male equivalent of *Loose Women*. It's because *Loose Men* would be awful. We've got thousands of podcasts for men to moan at the state of the world, but literally no one would want to hear one where they moaned about their wives. For all the Joe Rogans and Jordan Petersons of this world, tackling the difficulty that society has in accommodating typically masculine thinking, have you once heard them say, 'My partner hasn't been very nice to me recently'? And thus blokes are left a bit impotent in their facility to articulate what their love life is missing.

So let's talk about our marriages a bit more, but not too much. Let's compromise and discuss our relationships, but using the cryptic devices often deployed by politicians.

Instead of saying 'She's bleeding useless', like one of the Loose Women might happily say of their hapless fella, let's settle for a diplomatic, 'Lately things have been sub-optimal.' Other blokes will know what that understatement means without you

193

sounding like a scab crossing the marital picket line. And let's not go back to the old 'ball and chain' analogies of previous generations either.

I had an uncle who whenever he saw his new wife's name appear on his mobile would blow his cheeks out and say, 'Uh-oh, the Fuhrer calls.'

Was it politically correct? No.

Was it funny? Sort of, but there has to be a middle ground between moaning about 'er indoors constantly and never moaning at all.

HEROES OF BLOKEDOM #4: PETER CROUCH

Reporter: What do you think you'd have been if you weren't a footballer?
Peter Crouch: A virgin.

I don't know if there's ever been any other quote that has so quickly identified someone as a good bloke. It has everything. Not only does Peter Crouch's answer turn the exchange into a proper joke, with the rhythm of set-up and punch, but more importantly, it's underlined by a rare level of self-awareness. In an era when young footballers spend as much time being media drilled as they do completing shuttle runs, in two words, Crouch identifies himself as an actual person. As a normal bloke, and a self-deprecating one at that.

Since he went into a post-football career of presenting and punditry, we've forgotten the charm that opened up those career possibilities for Peter in the first place. The famous 'virgin' quote wasn't his only zinger either.

In a reference to his looming six-foot-seven frame, Peter once claimed he was 'five foot nine at birth'. Answering a question as to why he hadn't joined the trend of footballers getting tattoos, he explained it was because 'none of my limbs are wide enough to support a visible image'.

All of these sound like the kind of retort you learn through the crucible of dressing-room banter. The best kind of defence mechanism is always to pre-empt criticism and get ahead of it. Peter was doing the football equivalent of Eminem's character at the end of *Eight Mile* when he takes on his detractors by listing every single one of his perceived weaknesses. Crouch was effectively rapping, 'I *am* really tall, I *do* have skinny limbs, my wife probably wouldn't have liked me if I'd been working on the bins.'

Crouch was also famous for the ironic 'robotics' goal celebration, which spawned a thousand substandard stag-do imitations. Such was his ability to land memorable moments in the public psyche that many people think it was Crouch's usual response to scoring. In fact, he only did it twice: once in 2006 playing for England against Jamaica and then a second and final time when he netted his hundredth Premier League goal. If you watch that moment back, the cheer when he reprises the robot is up there with the noise for the goal itself. The fans lucky enough to be present were smart enough to realise that they were seeing something special, the football equivalent of Springsteen getting back with the E Street Band.

All this self-awareness must have been something the young Peter Crouch had to master pretty quickly in the world of football because his size and frame would've marked him out for attention. In his early career, the terrace catcalls tended to either compare him to Rodney from *Only Fools and Horses* or – worse still – he had to endure thousands of grown men chanting 'freeeeak'. It's unfortunate, but that's football; any perceived weaknesses will duly have vinegar rubbed into that paper cut. And not only by the opposition fans.

In the late 1980s, my team, Wimbledon, had a player called Alan Cork who'd gone prematurely bald in his late twenties. We used to chant, 'Alan Cork, Alan Cork, Alan Alan Cork, he's got no hair but we don't care, Alan Alan Cork.'

Why were we playing mind games against one of our own players? We brought up his baldness but quickly countered that we were fine with it. If we were fine with it then why bring it up in the first place? We sounded like a wife subtly trying to initiate a dialogue about her husband getting hair replacement therapy.

Above all, Peter Crouch's humour showed intelligence, which was both everyday yet uncommon. Conscious footballers are all the rage now but back then, answering questions with more than one syllable could get you a reputation as a maverick.

Before Crouch, winger Pat Nevin had been seen as an oddity at Chelsea, not just because he looked like the guitarist in a New Romantic band but also because he'd been rumoured to read the odd broadsheet. A few years later, Graeme Le Saux, also of Chelsea, was subject to awful homophobic provocation by Robbie Fowler in a game against Liverpool. Piers Morgan speculated that no one really cared if he was gay (he isn't), the bigger problem was that he'd been known to read the *Guardian*. I'm not sure about that, but letting his smarts be known certainly didn't help.

Somehow, Peter Crouch managed to pull off wearing his intelligence on his sleeve without being persecuted for it, like his predecessors. Quite a feat.

When the Lad Lads Lads nineties morphed into the Wag Wags Wags excesses of the noughties, it sometimes felt like Crouch was the one guy in the England team who didn't take himself seriously – even if he had pulled a tabloid-approved 'stunner' in Abbey Clancy.

If anything, a thoughtful figure like Peter Crouch might be more at home playing right now, at a time when footballers are just as likely to be on the phone to Unicef as they are to their bookies, and the only girls invited back to Marcus Rashford's hotel room would be to balance the gender diversity in his and Kieran Trippier's book club.

The tribal nature of football can often bring out the worst in fans and players alike. Where fans tend to shout abuse, sometimes a modern player's first thought when celebrating a goal is to run the length of the field to do that awful 'shushing' thing. The joy on Peter Crouch's face when he scored, however, always seemed a lot closer to any normal bloke having a kickabout down the park with his mates. His success seemed as much of a pleasant surprise to him as it did to everyone else.

Peter Crouch had great gifts but they were delivered in an unlikely lanky package.

Blokeiness can demand a degree of conformity but, equally, nothing wins the respect of the group quicker than resolutely being yourself.

He had the good grace to acknowledge he was unusual and in the face of relentless banter and abuse, he stood tall.

Very, very tall.

THE BIG ONE (OR THE AVERAGE ONE, FOR MOST OF US)

The average erect penis in the UK is 5.17 inches.

So here it is. In many ways THE subject. The big one. Or the small one. Or the average one, depending how nature treated you.
Penis size.

An ex-girlfriend once said to me, 'You're a lot more interested in penises than I am.'

As a heterosexual man, it was an odd thing to hear, but undeniably true. Bluntly put, men know a lot more about willies than women ever will.

We own one. We have, through the process of sport and shared locker rooms, seen more penises than the average woman. We know more about their sizes and shapes but admittedly a lot less about how they look up-close and erect (unless you were *very* close team-mates).

For a long time, women's inferior knowledge wasn't helped by the lack of willies in films and television shows. The balance has been redressed somewhat by the Channel 4 show *Naked Attraction* (which, let's be honest, could've been called 'Who wants to look at some dicks?'). Though that programme hasn't exactly enhanced the brand of the male genitalia. The penis wasn't particularly aesthetically pleasing in the first place, let alone when stood exposed in a neon Perspex box, teased by a prior peak at some bloke's hairy shins.

No matter how many dicks have been available in popular culture, for all blokes, there will have been a point where they'll have considered their own penis and wondered, 'What's mine like? How does it compare?'

Are you a grower or a shower? Have you been cursed by the gods or gifted? Or are you, like almost every single bloke on the planet, making your way in the middle lane of member mediocrity?

I'm not sure exactly when I first became conscious of the existence of very large penises. I do, however, remember sitting with my then girlfriend one night watching *The Word* on Channel 4 in the mid-nineties. The programme showed an interview with the porn star Jeff Stryker. He was wearing cycling shorts and his manhood seemed to be resting somewhere just above his knee (what is it with Channel 4 and knobs? Was showing some one of the public service remits when the channel first acquired its licence?). I looked at my girlfriend, tried to gauge how she was responding, and sensibly concluded she could only be thinking that mine was now completely unsatisfactory and her only realistic option was to leave me, head to Vegas and set up a new life with this Stryker fellow.

It might've been a slight over-reaction on my part but the experience did speak to something I hadn't realised I'd internally concluded: women are drawn to men with larger penises.

Cards on the table: I have, like most blokes, measured my own penis and everything comes in around the average. I could add euphemistically that I've 'never had any complaints', but it would be a particularly cruel woman who would finish having sex then hop straight onto DickAdvisor to administer a withering two-star review.

Most blokes are aware that consistent majorities of women claim that size makes no difference to sexual fulfilment. But what if the majority of women are simply being nice? *Maybe* the third of women in a survey with Dating Advice who said a longer than average penis does improve sex are the honest ones? Or maybe they have larger vaginas? And why are these studies always about length rather than girth? It's like talking about a car's top speed without considering miles per gallon.

While women are judged more overtly and frequently about how they look, penis size is the one anxiety many blokes carry around with them, however irrational it may be.

I've spoken with blokes my age to try to work out where this self-doubt comes from (conversations which, as you might guess, prompted them to assume I was hung like a strawberry on a bird's nest). One thing that did come up was a glut of 'dick-shaming' in the nineties. Several of us could recall that gesture women would often use to emasculate a guy – the one where they'd hold up their little finger derisively.

There was also a song around that time called 'Short Dick Man' by 20 Fingers, which somehow got radio play. The song includes some charming lyrics, including asking if the imaginary man needed tweezers to put that thing away and inviting him to 'put his pants back on' and depart (the polite translation). Harsh enough, but there's also public record on YouTube of that song being performed on kids' TV. I don't know what happened to the boys who were in that studio audience, but I'm guessing some of them break into a cold sweat at the sight of tweezers.

Women might counter that boob size is an equivalent point of concern, but while fun, breasts aren't directly involved in the experience of penetrative sex. And if women are really anxious about cup size, they have, finances allowing, the option of doing something about it. Despite all the advances in surgery, there are no reliable procedures to enhances penises. The ones that exist all seem to leave it looking a cauliflower which got run over by a tractor. So for now, penis size is another bodily feature, like height, which men can do nothing about. Believe me, if there was an exercise which blokes could do to increase their size we'd be down that gym day and night.

Big penises also have mystical cultural power, so much so that we all know about the well-hung men of history, like Errol Flynn, Milton Burrell and Rasputin.

Rasputin's large member was so feted that some refused to believe it had died with him and came up with a lurid tale whereby it was kept in a box and handed around women in Russian high society (though the thing they were passing around was most likely to be a dried-up sea cucumber – which itself sounds like an unflattering euphemism).

The penis is seen as a vestige of your masculinity; it's even called your 'manhood'. Additionally, we now have a new name for the inner confidence of the well-hung man: 'BDE', meaning 'big dick energy'. That quiet self-belief which emanates from knowing at least one part of your body could elicit gasps from a crowd.

All of this speaks to the idea that our virility and reputation as a lover is bound up with the proportions of our genitals. Perhaps that's why some women choose to mock and humiliate, because, for all men's perceived power, the penis acts like nature's Achilles' heel.

The words around penis size seem to imply the idea of quasi-religious interventions. 'Well-hung' implies a gift from the gods. 'Blessed', 'well endowed', 'first in the queue' all make it sound like Mother Nature did you a solid.

A large schlong can, however, be a mixed blessing. Some particularly well-hung men suffer issues sustaining erections and others report dizzy spells while aroused. To my unevolved bloke brain, though, that still sounds like boasting. 'Lads, it's so big that if I get a boner I have to have a sit down.' It could be classed as a nice problem to have, like complaining about how much it costs to heat your swimming pool.

If you're in the absolute top tier of willies, it must be an interesting life. According to *Everyday Health*, only 16 per cent of men have a penis longer than six inches. Anything significantly above that and your gift is so statistically rare that it must feel like a kind of superpower. You're a Marvel hero who can only strap on his cape during the rare occasions you're having sex.

In my experience, most blokes in this elite category will find a way of letting you know they're well-hung. Sometimes they'll just straight out tell you. Or they'll get drunk and produce it on a stag-do. And who can blame them? If it was me, I might like everyone to know I was Superman rather than plain old Clark Kent.

Forty-five per cent of men were dissatisfied with the size of their penis, despite only 16 per cent being shorter than the average range – which means the vast majority of men's anxiety is entirely irrational. However, all the things said to reassure men about the size of their manhood sound suspect at best and patronising at worst.

'It's not the size of the ship, it's the motion of the ocean'.

That sounds suspiciously like something your nan would tell you, up there with your mum assuring you that when you get older there'll be girls 'queuing around the block'.

You can't help but wonder: 'What if your ocean had great motion AND a massive ship?'

Early in their lives, blokes are wired to think that big is good. Big planes, big trucks, big rockets – consequently, it's very difficult to imagine that not being able to do a proper 'windmill' is somehow an advantage. But as blokes age, we reconcile ourselves to our place in the scheme of life generally, not least where we fit into the global dick index.

And if you're still harbouring a lifelong grievance that you weren't one of the penile 1 per cent a further consolation is that once you get into late middle age you realise the former legends of the locker room aren't able to give their hardware a run-out as often as they used to. By that point, with tiredness and reduced libido bearing down on their sex lives, it must be like having an expensive sports car they can't take out for a spin due to the rising price of fuel.

* With heavy irony, this chapter is almost the exact average length when compared to the others in the book.

WHY BLOKES KNOW BETTER THAN SAT NAV

Up and down Britain, on the motorways and B roads, many blokes are locked in an ongoing and bitter dispute. It's not with their wives, partners or even their kids. It's with the technology they're using to get where they need to be: the sat nav. It might be generational – young men may have evolved to accept technology's judgement more willingly – but there's something about the mindset of many blokes which leads them to think that the sat nav is some kind of malevolent sleeper cell trying to destroy their life.

It's not just the conviction that I know better; as a bloke, I believe the sat nav is actively out to thwart me.

A few years ago, I was on the A14 (solid road) heading from west to east when the device told me to come off at a junction and take the third exit on the roundabout and join the dual carriageway . . . which brought me straight back onto the A14.

OK, that might not be the most exciting line you've read in a book this year, but it was one of these tedious travel developments that, while no one else gives a toss about it, when it happens to you, you deem it worthy of a phone call to your wife to relay this latest outrage.

Have you had this feeling you're being tooled with by technology? Or are you still evaluating my assessment of the A14 as a 'solid road'? That's because your proper bloke will always have an opinion on the big travel infrastructure.

On my last tour, I posed a regular question to some of the boomer generation men in the audience. I asked them what their biggest childhood fear was. Most replied 'nothing', 'I don't know' or something weird like 'wild dogs'. However, when I followed up by asking them their favourite motorway service station every single one of them answered in a heartbeat (a lot of love for Tebay service in Cumbria, if you're interested; personally I'm more of a Beaconsfield man myself). I do love a service station. The modern versions have evolved and many now contain pubs, a Pizza Express and, in some cases, a Nando's. They're practically resorts (though I might stop short of suggesting to my wife that we spend next Easter at Leigh Delamere). The fact I feel so at home in places designed for people between places is probably another one for the counsellor.

Going back to sat nav – my aversion to it isn't just my own misplaced male pride. As previously discussed, I often find driving to be a pleasure, so the idea of spending every single journey constantly waiting for a disembodied female voice to alert me to the next junction is another example of drawing too keenly on the teat of technology. It plays into my fear that while masculinity is evolving rapidly, some of the good things about being a bloke are being washed away with the bath water. It might be a ball-ache to work out a route before you set off, but at least you can get your head up and actually take in where you're going.

I've got a mate who's been working at a call centre since Covid and he follows the sat nav's directions every single day. Maybe it's a form of quasi-meditation, where being told 'in 200 yards, take the next left' is a way of realigning his chakras, but he's a disgrace and is lucky I still talk to him.

Being a stand-up comedian and always on the road, I know how to get to most major towns and cities in the UK without even consulting a map (yes, another medal is probably in order). Not only that, I can tell you which services have a KFC, which have Burger King and all the ones that have those weird vending machines which dispense disposable toothbrushes. My hope is that by the time my son becomes an adult, my extraordinary directional sense will rank me somewhere between Bear Grylls and a sorcerer.

It all comes from a belief that I shouldn't need help with directions. In my childhood, before the advent of sat nav, I wasn't the only one who heard his mum implore his dad to just 'pull over and ask for directions'. This never felt like a great option, not least because the chances of the locals knowing anything about where they live tended to be pretty low. Not only do you undergo the emasculation of being lost you have to endure someone else going through their own personal shame when – despite having lived in a place for thirty years – they can't tell you how to get from the train station to the leisure centre. Or they know their town too well and think they can impart that wisdom by plotting a route using landmarks only a lifelong local would know – 'Turn left by the growers farm, carrying on past the bombed-out bus shelter then pull up by Dave the tramp.'

Since the arrival of Uber and a generally more professional brand of taxi driver, a further dimension of directional arrogance has emerged as the driver will often ask if you have a 'preferred route'. My wife cringes at this as she knows I'll launch into my pet subject of why the M25 is actually a better bet late at night, providing there are no roadworks. Still, it's better that they ask rather than blithely accept what sat nav offers up, leaving me scowling on the backseat, asking loaded rhetorical questions like, 'You sure the A1 is the best option? Nope, *you're the professional* . . . all I'm saying is that crossroads around Fiveways corner can get *pretty* congested around this time of night.'

Navigation is something I expect to form part of my narrow repertoire of blokey skills. It's an important USP for men, as there aren't many areas in which we demonstrably outperform females. In aptitude tests, there's almost no area where young boys exceed their female counterparts, apart from the ability to mentally rotate images. This suggests that males may have a slight edge on working out how to get places (or why we were better at Tetris).

The unfortunate flipside, however, is that now most smartphones have effective map applications, once we get universal 5G, men may become completely obsolete.

'A man who doesn't spend time with his family can never be a real man.'

Don Corleone,
The Godfather

SPORTING HOLY TRINITY #3: DARTS

'Stand up if you love the darts.'
(Most common chant at darts events.)

I do, indeed, 'love the darts'.

If you're a rugby fan reading this, please don't be offended that your sport didn't make the cut for the holy trinity of sports. I accept that, nationally, the three premier sports in Britain would generally be perceived to be cricket, football and rugby. I respect rugby but I can't shake off the sense that it's a load of emotionally repressed men finding an excuse to hug for eighty minutes. And I know no one actually says 'rugger' any more but I also can't shake off the peculiar class-based hives that word brings me out in. Even if rugby is played extensively in Wales and Hull, I can't quite escape the idea that everyone on the pitch knows which knife to use for fish. I was also never sold on the idea that all of rugby's violence is completely excused by the fact that they call the referee 'sir'. It's like trying to avoid getting a prison sentence for armed robbery because you were polite to the arresting officer.

Darts, on the other hand, is the most supreme of blokeish pursuits. Most sports aren't things you could do in your house. Snooker and pool tables are not things the majority of people have the space for. But if you have a dartboard and the length of an oche available, you're playing exactly the same sport as the true greats of the game. A 180 scored at the Lakeside requires the same technical proficiency as one scored in the garage of a two-bed semi (though you might have slightly fewer blokes in Super Mario fancy dress singing in the background).

My mum used to love watching darts, back in the eighties, a time of huge viewing figures and household names like 'Crafty Cockney' Eric Bristow and 'Jocky' Wilson. Apart from wrestling, this was the only sport in Britain where the 'athletes' had nicknames. Or where the athletes looked nothing like athletes. The sight of men drinking and smoking their way through high-level competitions made the game look like a world I was used to. The wood panelling, the burgundy carpets – all of the big tournaments seemed to take place in venues which looked like my dad's local.

By the time I first went to the darts in the mid-noughties, things had changed. The first thing you need to understand is that I went to '*the* darts', the proper one, the BDO at Lakeside, not the glitzy PDC version at Ally Pally, which you might have seen on Sky Sports. It had barely evolved from the sport I watched on telly as a child. The venue was now smoke-free but in its place was the thick smell of stodgy fried food. The grub was so heavy that if you'd had five pints plus their pie and mash it would take its toll. During the mid-evening session, you'd see hundreds of blokes asleep in the background like they'd been shot with an elephant dart.

The Lakeside venue itself reminded me of an eighties caravan park. The walls were adorned with various big showbiz names who'd performed there in the past. I'm talking big hitters. Carolgees, Norman Wisdom, Duncan Norvelle and Sinitta. The whole place was stuck in a comforting time warp. Though they'd made one or two concessions to modernity. Now all of the players had nicknames rather than just a select few. Some were more organic than others. I never really understood the point of Ted

'The Count' Hankey, other than that he was a bit creepy and threw out some toy bats on his way to the oche.

Over the years, the BDO standard didn't keep up with its more illustrious and financially backed glitzy rival (the breakaway PDC), but, in a way, that was part of the charm. You'd see a guy called something like Steve 'Sizemic' Southern appear from the dressing room amid a sea of lasers and dry ice. As Steve 'Sizemic' bopped out to the strains of 'Cotton-Eyed Joe', you'd realise that the nickname was more a comment on his BMI than on his darts ability. Nonetheless, it was great to see an ordinary bloke who looked like he drove a van get his moment in the sun.

The quality of the darts was helpful but not essential. Darts is a brilliant game because it's always moving forwards, and even if two cloggers eventually end up chasing a double one for half an hour you can take refuge in gallows humour.

Rather than supporting one or other player, people who go to darts tend to support 'the darts'. If you watch highlights of great matches on YouTube you'll see fans cheering a 180 by one bloke then cheering even more if the next bloke does the same. It's all about the love of the game, arguably more so than cricket. The competitors might come second but the supporters never do. You might support Neil 'Duffman' Duff but if he lost to Thibault 'The French Touch' Tricole you'd still come away happy if it had been a good match. You can't lose as a darts spectator; it's like an each-way bet on the boat race.

Hence one of the most popular chants is 'stand up if you love the darts'. No one watching their favourite football team getting a hiding has ever tried to get their fans doing a conga for the sheer love of the game.

I have dabbled with the more glamorous PDC at Ally Pally. It was fun, but with all the razzmatazz I got the sense that the actual darts was more of a sideshow.

I attended with the comics Seann Walsh and Romesh Ranganathan. The fans, always on the scout for new and interesting banter, spotted the infinitely better-known Romesh and Seann and started having some fun. First they chanted 'Seann Walsh down a pint', which he did. Then they moved on to imploring Romesh to down a pint.

They must have spotted me looking left out and, somewhat charitably, followed up by singing, 'Comedian's mate, down a pint.'

It's that humour I love.

Despite that one flirtation with the big time, the BDO, with its darts purism and general sense of chintz, was always going to be my natural home.

However, in 2020, the BDO lost their minds and moved away from their spiritual home of the Lakeside and tried to set up at the snazzy Indigo at London's O2. They'd tried to keep up with the Joneses and it was a massive mistake. Crowds plummeted and the eventual winner ended up on less than a quarter of the tournament's usual prize pot. In the subsequent inquest as to how this had happened, many blamed not consulting with the players. I think they should've consulted with the fans. So much of life now occurs in these ubiquitous grey monoliths like the O2, with the usual array of Five Guys and Pizza Express, that a yearly trip to the Lakeside represented a stay against changing times. What could be more blokey than that?

The Lakeside still being the Lakeside was something you could rely on.

Pizza Express? That's something you do with the wife, but the

Lakeside had beer, crap food, bad decor, banter and – crucially –
it all felt like something you could have a go at, given half the
chance.

Despite large crowds of pissed-up working-class blokes, you
rarely get any crowd trouble at the darts because everyone's
supporting the same thing: having a laugh.

The only time there's a chance it might genuinely kick off is if
the bar shuts early.

DEVIL WOMAN

The British public's obsession with Harry and Meghan is a curious and much remarked upon thing. Most debates on the couple will eventually alight on the question of 'why do we care so much in the first place?'.

It's pretty simple. The change in Harry's personality is something we recognise from similar relationships involving men we know. We saw Harry as a good bloke, then he got married, started to change and seem like less of a laugh, so many of us concluded that it was all Meghan's fault.

But was it?

In any bloke's lifetime there will be several fellas who after meeting the love of their life, seem to shed their original skin, seemingly overnight. Often, that kind of bloke – let's call him 'Duncan' – has picked someone who doesn't easily fit in with the group. Consequently, there's chatter within the family unit, possibly even a breakaway WhatsApp group, raising the very real risk someone gets their groups wrong and accidentally posts something meant for the 'we hate Alison' chat to the main group.

It all kicks off. The family's very own John and Yoko stop showing up for get-togethers.

Duncan then becomes outspoken on issues he previously didn't care about.

One of my most voracious meat-eating mates suddenly became a vegan two months after moving to Scotland with his new Mrs, who just happened to be vegan. There were numerous sightings of him at late-night drive-thru KFCs, but he became very defensive when those meat-free credentials were questioned in front of his new lady (even if he had just been for a random drive and was clearly fighting the meat sweats).

But does this analysis of the manipulated man fall into well-worn clichés around female manipulation, stretching right back to Adam and Eve? If your view about the male–female dynamic is traditional you could credit that theory, especially when you factor in the beauty of the bloke's new partner.

Meghan is a good example in this respect, as she's very good-looking and – superficial or not – this matters. Let's put a number on it: she's a nine and Harry is a six. Don't feel bad for Harry; historically speaking, those are pretty strong numbers for a ginger (sorry, I'm a stand-up, had to do a ginger slam – union rules). When you factor in Harry's general princelyness that could drag his average up at least another half point.

Despite the dream of every bloke to be punching above his weight, if you punch too far you could end up with a skewed power dynamic which takes the relationship to strange places. Taking the fighting/punching analogy further, Meghan is MMA while Harry's playing thumby wars. We've all seen this dynamic up close.

Growing up, everyone had that pal who liked a beer, played the field and was squarely one of the lads. A Duncan.

Then one fateful night he meets Alison.

You can tell from the first minute that Alison has changed him. Even when she comes over to say hello to his mates she is already suggesting that 'maybe he should have a soft drink this round'. This guy always used to be on the dancefloor singing all the words to 'Jump Around' but now he's looking on like a teacher monitoring the sixth-form disco.

Over the next few weeks and months, you don't see much of your mate Duncan. When you do see him something's clearly changed. He's a bit on the serious side these days. He's backtracked on the lads' holiday and is now saving up for a trip with Alison, which involves some sinister activity called 'sightseeing'. On the odd occasion he does come out, Alison has developed the ability to control him merely using her eyes. Simple movements left to right or up and down can get him to do things, as they indicate which activities he shouldn't take part in.

Then you finally get Duncan out for a lads-only night. He arrives to the pub late (the group have already speculated that she's deployed some last-minute psych-ops to get him to cancel). It's clear on entrance that he's been comprehensively restyled. He's wearing white chinos, a black turtleneck and stinks of Issey Miyake (it's the nineties in this story, but that's context rather than a legitimate excuse).

The black turtleneck is a big giveaway. I don't know any bloke who has willingly put on that garment unless he was relaunching himself as a philosopher or tech wizard. Duncan is also sporting a new hairdo which is, frankly, a bit on the busy side. You can see as he shuffles his way across to you that, deep within, he knows he's let himself – and the entire bloke brotherhood – down.

It's quiet as he sits. Everyone is trying to work out what they can say to this poor fella who seems to have come to a fancy dress party dressed as a knob. Ultimately, the group opts for the simplest line of attack: the black turtleneck. There are several variations on the Milk Tray theme (remember, this is pre-Steve Jobs).

Eventually, Duncan flips: 'You know what? Fuck you lot. You're so immature [bear in mind he's twenty at this point and was doing bunny hops just the other week]. I'm going round Alison's; we've got an early start tomorrow.'

Everyone nods and goes quiet. We can only hope that the early start isn't for a spa day.

OK. There's a chance that those experiences were underscored by sexist presumptions. Duncan might have actually *wanted* early nights and giant dressing gowns. The turtleneck could also have been his idea (doubt it, but we can't rule it out). And so, too, we have to concede that Harry might not simply be under some sort of trance-like spell from the 'evil' Meghan.

The idea of a man re-evaluating a family culture which involves briefing to the press after Christmas dinner isn't that much of a long walk, especially when you factor in what happened to Harry's mother. In fact, taking into account his conviction that the British tabloid press indirectly killed his mum, if a story broke that someone had stolen an Apache helicopter and shot up the majority of British newspaper headquarters it would certainly be worth asking Harry where he was that afternoon.

It's hard, though. Just like with Duncan, we were all quite invested in Harry as a bloke. Who couldn't be after what happened to him at such a young age? No one who watched that poor lad trail behind his mother's coffin with his head bowed low could ever forget the consequences of what he was born into.

We followed his early 'jack-the-lad' romantic entanglements with interest. Many were sort of proud that he went on active service for the armed forces (rather than the cosmetic surface kind favoured by some of his relatives and ancestors). Most of us were eventually forgiving when we saw photos of him playing strip billiards in Vegas (it turns out that what happens in Vegas doesn't stay in Vegas if you're second in line to the throne).

The fundamental change in Harry's character speaks to what we know about certain blokes when they fall head over heels in love. They pick women who seem to want to de-bloke them. Women who drive them towards less time for hobbies, less time with the lads, and more time mooching around farmer's markets.

The impulse to change a man is hard for blokes to understand. Getting into a relationship with a woman is a much more linear thing. Blokes meet a woman, think 'I like her' and if they like her a lot they'll want to spend more and more time together. The process of whittling them down or improving them isn't something that generally occurs to most men. When it does, it seems to be the preserve of an extreme, controlling, small band of genuinely toxic pricks.

Conversely, we joke openly about women seeing men as a 'project'. I've got no issue with that, so long as it's a drive towards evolution rather than revolution. Not just because I want my mates to still come to the darts with me each year, but because I don't understand why a woman would settle down with a bloke she had so many issues with in the first place. If his grunting, drinking and watching sports bother you so much maybe he's not the guy.

None of this, however, changes the fact that it's ultimately the bloke's responsibility to either not couple up with a woman who wants to change him or admit to everybody that he knows which side his bread's buttered and is happy to go along with it for a quiet life. There are plenty of blokes who weigh up the domestic comforts afforded by being in a stable relationship and conclude that there's less to lose by becoming more distant from family and friends.

So let's stop blaming everything on the Meghans and Yokos (even the Alisons), and keep some space for the idea of holding men accountable for how they become separate from the people who've always loved them. This kind of dislocation happens because the bloke allows it. Even if the woman *is* on 'manoeuvres', they're grown men.

And if it really is a bad relationship, in the long run it will inevitably implode. The job of everybody else is to keep close enough to pick up the pieces if and when it does go tits up.

WHO NEEDS ABS ANYWAY?

Women can have visible abs with 14 to 20 per cent body fat, while men's needs to be as low as 6 to 13 per cent.

There comes a time in the life of most blokes when – like deciding you're going to learn a language, master the art of playing poker or brew your own beer – you decide you're going to develop abs.

You're going to get 'ripped'.

Even the language of getting fit is different for men and women. Women get in 'shape'; they 'tone up' or 'slim down'. Meanwhile, men get 'ripped' or 'shredded'. They 'monster their guns' and 'beast their pecs'. The feeling also persists that whatever issues exist in your life, whether they be mental, physical, career or relationship, they might all be solved by having washboard abs.

When I was young – certainly before the discussion about men's health and grooming evolved to where it is now – the belief lingered that abs were achievable through doing a few sit-ups every now and then. If a bloke did a hundred sit-ups a day for, say, I dunno, a week and a half, they'd be walking around looking like one of the Hemsworth brothers. One hundred sit-ups a day wouldn't have done anyone any harm, but most people came to understand that having abs is a bit more complicated than that.

Men might need to have as little as 6 per cent body fat for abs to even be visible. Imagine having just 6 per cent body fat and still not showing. It must feel like an oil exec knowing the volume of fossil fuels stashed beneath those pesky glaciers.

It's one of biology's few cruel tricks on men that women, who feel less societal compulsion to have visible abdominal muscles, can achieve them much more easily (however, given childbirth, menstruation and all the other stuff, maybe we can let that one go).

The bottom line is this: it's really *hard* to have a six-pack. So hard that when you think about movie action heroes or actors who spend their working day in capes, it's surprising how little they bitch about that requirement for the job. We hear a lot from actresses about the pressure for them to have a good body and look young, which is fair enough, but I can't recall a single interview where Robert Downey Jr sat and whinged about the need to still have groin cleavage well into his fifties. I don't recall a tearful Jason Statham chat where he detailed doing a savage bicep workout on two boiled eggs and a handful of chia seeds.

It's not just about being slim enough to have abs; most of these lads need to devote a daily couple of hours in the gym so they'll look like they'd have the upper-body strength to gut punch Thanos. The guns have to be spectacular, the chest like Kevlar, and the abs need to look sharp enough to grate cheese on.

If anyone in Hollywood should be moaning about oppressive ideas of physical perfection it should be the male cast of Marvel. But they don't because the broad idea that men are inherently privileged means we don't want to hear the rich Batman guy complaining about having to do squat thrusts or the mighty Superman whinging about a shoulder injury he sustained doing Tough Mudder.

It's not just superheroes either. A lot of people (me included) remember the shape Daniel Craig was in as he emerged from the sea in *Casino Royale* in *those* trunks. He was in such eye-catching physical condition that it was the first time I'd heard a bloke described as wearing 'those' anything. Finally, we had a male equivalent to Liz Hurley in 'that' dress. It's tempting to think Daniel Craig is just a naturally well-built fella, but his Bond-bod wasn't just a consequence of cutting back on the carbs or having slimline tonic with his Martini. Looking like that is a full-time job, one where you'd need to hit the gym most days in order to sculpt a physical ideal.

The multimillionaire gods of Hollywood may never moan about their lot, but just know that I see you, lads. I hope you feel seen. My wife has certainly seen you a lot and she likes what she sees.

Another aversion blokes have to abs arises from sheer pragmatism: once you know what it takes to have them, the ownership of a solid keg is an external acknowledgement of your vanity and need for approval. Other blokes will know it's not just dietary control and a bit of exercise: you've sacrificed large chunks of your life so that your stomach looks like an irrigated field in a dry country.

My suspicion of a strict fitness regime is that I've always been wary of any activity you literally *have* to adhere to. There's no room for vegging out or giving it a miss to watch golf all day. Some blokes watch sport in the gym but that's ruining a thing of beauty, like putting ketchup on curry.

The whole culture of the gym operates in a male sphere where I've never felt comfortable. The glossary of terms make me flinch in the same way 'rugger' does. 'Spotting', 'benching', 'power lifting'. It doesn't fit too well with the blokey drive towards not taking anything too seriously.

Also, gyms are like playing the one-armed bandit – you don't have to hang around one too long before someone starts giving you unsolicited advice. The most common one is that 'cardio isn't great for weight loss, dude, you should be pushing weights'. But I don't *like* pushing weights. I can just about tolerate a few bicep curls between the running and rowing machines. I do the cardio stuff because I like it and, afterwards, feel a bit better. I'd rather have to be winched out of my house for weight reasons than ever deadlift while keeping full eye contact with myself in the mirror. So you can be in terrific shape, but you might have to hand your bloke card back in. At least temporarily, like an MP declaring a conflict of interest.

The other issue with suddenly taking your image too seriously is that, if you're middle-aged and in a reasonably long marriage, the development of abs could – just like the flowers from the petrol station – be a cause for suspicion. Unless you've got a third audition for the *Avengers* reboot you might have to reassure your wife that you're not trying to impress some twenty-year-old in the office.

I've been between thirteen and thirteen and a half stone for about ten years now. I am overweight but, crucially (I tell myself), it's stable. Just like with my clothes, my wife knows what she's getting and throughout our relationship she's been in better shape than me. If I were to suddenly get ripped this may produce undue pressure on her to match me pound for pound. That's why I don't do weights – this kind of development at our time in life would be, frankly, ungentlemanly.

So when it comes to blokes getting abs, particularly middle-aged blokes, the advice is to go quietly into the night. Abs are a young man's game. Older blokes were lucky enough to be raised at a time when there was no such expectation for the vast majority of men. During an era when so much male privilege is being reassessed, that's a win you can take to the bank.

Instead of striving for something so hard, do personal work on how you see your belly. A slight paunch, rather than suggesting laziness or complacency, actually represents the acceptance of the passage of time. It's philosophically sound reasoning. Buddha had a little gut on him – and if it was good enough for Buddha it should be good enough for you.

WHAT GOES ON TOUR STRAYS ON TOUR

The average British man gets married at thirty-two.

Stag-dos are the gala dinner of being a bloke. Oddly, given their centrality to the male experience – and high billing on the rites of passage list – they tend to start happening relatively late in life.

Thankfully, things have moved on from the reckless former incarnation of stag-dos, which took place the night before the wedding. Some things which seem odd in retrospect might have made sense at the time (caning, smoking in cinemas, your doctor having a bottle of brandy under his desk) but I cannot fathom why getting monumentally hammered the night before your wedding was ever seen as a smart move. Perhaps, given that marriage was often spoken of in negative terms back then, with the implication that most marital unions were happening under duress, the pre-wedding drink-up may have felt akin to a condemned man being granted permission to drink himself to oblivion the night before facing the gallows.

The way men talk about marriage has changed a lot in a short space of time. I can still remember even into the early noughties crafty shouts of 'Don't do it!' in the church while waiting for the bride. Today's more emotionally in tune young men might shout 'don't do it' but only in relation to a poorly thought through shirt and tie combo.

There tends to be a glut of stag-dos around a bloke's early thirties. Most of the disposal income around this time gets gobbled up by raucous and expensive three-day jaunts. Men of this age know they should probably be saving up for a deposit on a house but instead find themselves throwing hundreds of pounds at easyJet and adult go-karts.

Like all aspects of the blokeosphere, your experience of stag-dos can vary wildly. Each stag-do has its own tone and I don't want to sound snobbish, but I'm glad I haven't yet been on one which involved the wearing of novelty T-shirts. You don't need a printed nickname to let strangers know who you are. If you are 'Shagmonster' or 'Gassy Gavin' all of that should become apparent soon enough. Though, in their defence, themed T-shirts might be a good way of keeping a large group visible and together, plus serve as reassurance for anxious partners back home that you look like such dickheads the only women who'll show an interest in you will be muggers.

Another interesting feature of a stag-do is you get to find out who your mate's other friends are. Luckily, with blokes, the jeopardy of crossing the friendship streams isn't quite as fraught as it can be for women, but it's still new territory. You can come to learn whether your friendship category is 'legacy' or 'aspirational'. It can be revealing too, as if you're a mate from way back, you see a different side of your pal around his new muckers and whether he's putting on airs and graces or this is just who he is now.

You can be surprised to find out that you're not even the most blokey group of friends he has. I have mates who most people would class as fairly route one, but on a stag-do a few years ago we felt like ladies-in-waiting compared to the other animals the stag had brought along. There will also be a level above the animals – the 'wrong 'un' mates. The group of legacy friends who aptly demonstrate why he moved to a different city.

British stag-dos seemed to reach a zenith just before the credit crunch. Jacked up on cheap borrowing, a strong pound and never-to-be-repeated budget flights, they went from a one-night trip to the local curry house, to Blackpool, then Prague, until finally you had mates pitching up in Vegas for a month. I don't have a verifiable number, but I'd imagine those epic overseas adventures resulted in a lot of postponed weddings, either by misadventure or the bloke deciding he wasn't ready for commitment and preferred to get a job working the door for Siegfried & Roy.

Whatever kind of stag you're on, a lot can be gleaned from that first stupid o'clock mustering at the airport. There are early acts of bravado which can set the tone.

I'll risk losing blokey points here but, despite my love of lager, I'm not into the early-morning pint with a fry-up. I'm all for drinking at unusual times, but I'm resolutely of the belief that the flavour of lager simply doesn't go that well with fried eggs and meat. There's going to be so much drinking you really don't need to douse a good breakfast with the taste of Carling. (You'd actually probably be better off with a sparkling wine – however, crazy talk like that could go down badly and you don't want to spend the next three days being called 'Patsy' in a hilarious reference to *Ab Fab*.)

There is a kind of man for whom the stag-do is the only time he fully comes alive. He's the same bloke who always turned up for Saturday-morning football still stinking of snakebite and boasting of the previous evening's sexual conquest. He'll arrive with his head bobbing back and forward like a hyperactive pigeon of manly fun, already talking loudly and calling anyone who doesn't want to do shots outside the airport Starbucks 'ladies'. You'd think this guy would be intolerable, but he serves a talismanic purpose in the early knockings and is often proved to be a massive lightweight when push comes to actual shove. The same guy who was downing pints at the airport Wetherspoons is usually missing the first dinner to nip back to the hotel to get his head straight.

Conversely, there will often be one guy on a stag-do who pretty much no one else knows. A friend of the groom's Mrs's sister's fella. This quiet mouse of the early capers will often be the session monster you have to bail out of the police station on Las Ramblas. A suburban Frank the Tank. Plus, he's lost his phone, so you have to go full Interpol while someone tries to work out how to contact and reassure his wife.

The activities on the stag often veer between those childish things you wouldn't be able to do in any other circumstance and a cartoon version of manliness you feel you have to adhere to. Where else could you take part in go-karting without children present and not get stared at like you're a weirdo?

On my stag-do, we booked a five-a-side pitch in Liverpool for the Saturday morning. It was one of the worst decisions I've ever made. Some of the lads hadn't got to bed until 6am but here we were running around with faces so red it looked like we'd been doing poppers.

Some activities can be more 'grown-up' and the kind of thing you'd only get to do in the context of a weekend away. Clay pigeon shooting has become popular in recent years. It's not my bag but it helps form the narrative of the trip. You'll have the guy you expected to do well but does badly, then the guy you thought would be crap but suddenly seems like he's ex-special forces.

Paintballing is also fairly popular. I've seen that game do weird things to men. It gives you a brief glimpse into what could happen if society crumbled and it turns out that some men are never happier than when safely ensconced in a foxhole trying to shoot their best mate in the balls.

If social media is anything to go by, British blokes do seem to be somewhere near the top of the league when it comes to going nuts on a stag-do. The Americans whoop a lot, but don't seem to last the pace when it comes to drinking. You'd think the concept of a stag-do might be a bit beneath the French, but if anything the language they use suggests they take it even more seriously. It's called '*l'enterrement de vie de garçon*', which roughly translates as the 'burial of the life of the boy' (alright lads, let's keep it light, eh?). However, that idea does tally with the principles of the first-known examples of stag-dos, which occurred in Sparta, where military comrades would feast and toast one another the night before their wedding. The groom would say farewell to the freedom of his bachelor life but swear continued allegiance to his comrades.

I'm not sure whether, for an increasingly childish adult population, anyone does suddenly grow up in the manner the Spartan stag-dos imply. You only have to look at the increasing number of men who have a games room and the growing popularity of 'adult daytime raves'.

Perhaps the enduring appeal of the stag-do is that most blokes never really grow up, we just pretend to. The stag-do is a place where, just for a couple of days, a bloke can stop pretending.

WE SHOULD TRY TO GET AHEAD OF THE TRAFFIC

One bona fide indisputable benefit of being a bloke is the capacity to wrap up any social interaction promptly without having to explain yourself. Whether it's a phone call with another bloke, a text exchange or even a friend's wedding, you can – when it's obvious the main business has been concluded – simply say, 'OK, bye now.'

The fade has many names, which often allude to nationality. The Irish exit. The French exit. We could just as easily call it 'the Bloke's exit'. Or 'Bloxit', except, instead of holding a referendum, you leave a boring Christening without uttering a word.

This capacity to call time on interactions has often perplexed and infuriated the women around me. They just don't get it and I wonder if they're a little envious at how uncomplicated our social lives can be. Their equivalent – a sudden goodbye to a female friend or leaving a hen-do without hugging every single person – can be taken as rudeness and fire the starting gun on several months of conflict.

One of the most perilous spheres of female communication is the WhatsApp group for a hen-do. I've heard of all manner of thermonuclear eruptions in this context, as competing whims can be subject to the most forensic misreadings.

Stag-do planning tends to come from the opposite place, more like a benevolent dictatorship where it's widely accepted that one bloke is totally in charge. We all accept that being in control of such a thing is a massive ball-ache none of us really wanted so we will – to the best of our ability – simply consent to whatever plans are put in front of us (providing they're not illegal . . . in the country we're doing them, anyway). Any attempt to create fuss in the planning process will likely trigger a group roasting where you may be compared to notable divas from the world of showbiz. Even people being slightly late with their replies, or slow in transferring their monetary contribution to paintballing, can result in some fairly direct rebukes: 'You lazy pricks ANSWER THE FUCKING MESSAGES' or 'SORRY, HAVE I GOT TO REMORTGAGE JUST SO YOU TWATS CAN GO PAINTBALLING?'

I can't speak for all – or indeed any – female WhatsApp groups, but I do have a hunch that any message which started 'Where's my money you lazy bitches?' would spawn several breakout chats.

Anyway. When we go and visit friends, my wife's approach to calling time on the visit is completely different from mine.

I'll have often spent twenty minutes thinking, 'Well, this feels like it's done', but, having previous offences on my charge-sheet for prematurely thinking things are 'done', I hold off for as long as I can.

Eventually, my wife will give me 'the eyes', which indicates that, despite her greater sociability and social decency, she too thinks it's 'done' and departure is imminent (either that or she just can't be arsed with me moaning because we've hit the worst traffic on the westbound stretch of the M25). She'll exchange those coded signals which all parties recognise to be a sign that things are drawing to close, such as 'What are you guys up to tomorrow?' which can often mean 'When can we fuck off today?'

Then she'll sigh expansively and say, 'Annnnyway, we'd best be going.'

At this point, I make my first mistake by standing up far too quickly and saying, 'Yes!' Sensing I might have appeared too keen, I qualify that with, 'I mean, yes, in the sense of getting ahead of the traffic.'

I'll barely disguise my glee as I go on to talk warmly about the value of avoiding the traffic on the westbound stretch at this time. Then I stop talking. Then something odd happens.

Nothing happens.

Both the women remain seated. Perhaps embarrassed by the clunking unsubtlety of my desire to do one, my wife might start another conversational thread – 'Did you hear back about Danielle's situation with the school?'

At this point, I'm in trouble because I've already stood. I've played my hand. I can't sit down again because I'd be seen to endorse anything up to a further forty-five minutes of chat. However, I can't risk being even ruder than I've already been by tapping my watch and saying, 'Babe, I thought you said we were going?'

So, after a couple of minutes standing in the middle of someone else's lounge like human furniture, I say, 'I'll grab the coats!' I even throw in a toilet pit stop on the way just to give them even more time to wrap up the chat.

I get back into the lounge, with the coats under my arm like the maître d' at a fancy restaurant. But they're still seated. At this point, I drift into an odd twilight zone. I've gone all in and have no cards left to play so I stand there like a tool.

You start wondering whether they hatched some plan while you were getting the coats: 'Let's see how long we can make this idiot stand there, to teach him a lesson.'

Even as you're finally waving goodbye at the door, another conversation crops up.

You try to understand. They're more invested while in each other's company so perhaps it just takes longer to unravel that process. But you're anxious too as you sense that your standing holding coats, sighing like a bored eight-year-old, may not have gone unnoticed and could be a topic of 'discussion' on the way home.

But none of it matters. You take the punishment, she eventually sighs and you move towards the car door. Everyone now thinks you're a dick, and not without justification, but more importantly, you have beaten the worst of the traffic.

'He's just a man . . . be more man than him.'
Apollo Creed, *Rocky III*

HERO DAYDREAMS

Ten per cent of British men think they could beat a chimpanzee in a fight with their bare hands.

There's long been a stat doing the rounds which claims that men think about sex once every seven seconds. I've always been a bit doubtful about this. It doesn't allow nearly enough other time for all the other silly bollocks blokes routinely contemplate.

One mental preoccupation I've never seen much written about is our tendency for hero daydreams.

A recent poll by YouGov suggested that 34 per cent of British men felt they could land an aeroplane with no training, but with the qualifier that they'd have some support from air traffic control (the figure for women was half that).

I like the caveat about air traffic control, which seems to suggest: 'Hey, we're not saying we wouldn't need *any* support. It's not like we're *deluded*.'

For some reason, there's a part of the blokey psyche which needs to believe that when the shit hits the fan and the hero's call to action sounds we will undoubtedly rise to the moment (probably in slow motion, with really cool music playing in the background, barely flinching at a large explosion behind us).

Landing planes isn't the only high-pressure situation where many blokes back themselves. Just under 10 per cent of British blokes think they could win a fight with a chimpanzee. Get real, fellas. We've all been to the zoo. Having seen the upper-body strength of those lads as they swing effortlessly from tyre to tree, there's no doubt in my mind that – in the event of a man vs chimp conflict – my swaying dad bod wouldn't give the alpha male too many sleepless nights.

It's not just the contrast in general physical condition – animals fight differently. They don't run their actions through a rational prism, wondering if they'll get arrested or thinking, 'Will this inflame my carpal tunnel?' In the world of fight or flight, they don't leave anything on the table. Forget chimps, even a badger with nothing to lose could pose a formidable opponent.

Around 13 per cent of men think they could beat a large dog in a fight. I have some form in this matter. When my cockapoo, Lilly (you shuddup, it IS a manly breed), was about six months old I was out walking her when I spotted coming towards me a man who seemed like he might be a little bit drunk, which at midday on a Tuesday wasn't a promising sign. Another red flag was the fact that he had a Staffordshire bull terrier by his side and the dog wasn't on a lead (I know there are many people who love Staffies and will defend them to their dying day, but the breed has 'form' – all dogs can have a bad day at the office, but when Staffies do it's backed up by three stone of muscle and teeth). The man suddenly put his arm out to the side and the dog promptly sat down, so I thought, 'Fair play, it's clearly a well-trained dog', and felt guilty about my prior 'breedism'.

Then the fella walked off and the dog didn't follow. *It wasn't his dog.* The hand gesture and the dog sitting was mere coincidence.

The Staffie was now looking at my diminutive Lilly like she was either an enemy or lunch. Suddenly, it started attacking her; at one point, it had Lilly's whole head in its mouth. I tried to intervene and ended up on the ground wrestling with the two of them. I eventually got the dog's jaw free and Lilly ran across the road into a neighbour's garden. I was left holding the Staffie around the neck when it slowly turned to look at me, but luckily it didn't have the taste for man flesh that day.

It broke free and chased Lilly into the garden. I followed in hot but reluctant pursuit. I spent several minutes trying to get between the Staffie and my precious Lilly. (I've tried to block it out now, but I think I was screaming my dog's name in a very high-pitched voice. I've often wondered what this must've looked like to passing drivers. The grass in the garden was high and they may well have only seen a deranged-looking man hopping about shouting the word 'Lilly!' like a mad horticulturalist.)

I was eventually able to scoop up my poor terrified pooch and started walking away. The Staffie was hectoring me in that manic way feral bullies do once they've tasted blood. I eventually walked past a car wash and told the staff what was happening and left the beast to them (God knows what I expected them to do with it). I strode off with Lilly in my arms. Even though I'd been screeching (and possibly crying a bit), my mind's eye had rendered me as Bruce Willis in *Die Hard*.

I got Lilly home and thought she might be traumatised so should probably see a vet. The vet checked her out and reassured me that she was fine. I had a few cuts and bruises, but, moreover, was wide-eyed and still shaking.

The vet smartly realised who really needed attention.

'Are you OK, Mr Norcott?'

'I'm fine,' I replied too quickly, 'I'm just worried about Lilly.'

She nodded, then asked me to sit down and went to make

tea – with several sugars in (a part of the story I'd never share with my mum).

I still proudly sport a scar on my left wrist from this encounter (sadly for the purposes of my hero delusions, it wasn't from hand-to-paw combat with the dog, but from contact with the pavement I launched my thirteen-stone frame onto).

The truth was, Bruce Willis was nowhere to be seen.

Maybe it's all the superhero films we watch growing up, but the idea of saving everybody is intoxicating. I remember when I was in Afghanistan entertaining the troops (I don't like to bring it up) (I won a medal) (five tours) (three of which were on forward bases) I was on a Chinook which was circling high above Helmand province, as there had been reports of hostile activity below.

My mind went to a very strange place.

During the time we were circling, I engaged in one of the most ridiculous daydreams I've ever had. I imagined the Chinook got hit and we went down in enemy territory. Not only would I survive, I'd somehow seize the rear gunner position and provide covering fire for the RAF mechanics as they tried to get the aircraft going.

This is deluded enough in itself (I might not even have had the upper-body strength to remove the safety catch) but the worst of the narcissism centred on what would happen after we were rescued. I'd nobly refuse to take any public credit for my act of heroism. I actually played out myself shunning the Dictaphones of assembled reporters at RAF Brize Norton upon my return, choosing instead to run towards my family.

My daydream was punctured when real-world Geoff was still in that Chinook and had become so dizzy with all the circling that he needed to be violently sick in a soldier's helmet.

The truth is, blokes never grow up, so hero daydreams are a natural legacy of our flights of fancy as small boys.

I remember watching the first *Superman* film: the costume, that theme tune, the modest way he'd never take any credit, the fact that even the bad girls loved him too. I'd secretly pull my shirt open the way Superman did. There was also something intoxicating about the Clark Kent/Superman dichotomy. It planted in young boys' minds that no matter how plain or nerdy you might seem, there was a lot more going on beneath.

Sadly, that was where the cultural parallels ended.

One implication of American cinematic dominance is that the superheroes we worship all tend to roll their Rs. There are barely any British superheroes (with the honourable exception of Bananaman). The closest we come are guys like James Bond and Sherlock Holmes. Which makes sense, as if there was such a thing as a British superpower it would almost certainly be sardonic wit. Plus, I'm not sure the Americans have ever heard of 'Mondeo Man'.

Recently, I got to be the hero and protector I've always hoped I would, should the moment arise. Maybe not enough to earn the Victoria Cross, but good enough for me.

I'd taken my son to watch AFC Wimbledon playing Colchester away on 27 December 2022. We were sitting behind the goal and the players were warming up. They were pinging the ball pretty hard and several shots had already seen fans diving for cover. I thought about a couple of viral clips I'd seen of dads at baseball matches who, when the ball was coming towards them, had selfishly got out of the way and allowed the ball to smash into their partner or child. What an awful thing to exhibit – to demonstrate to the world that, when it mattered, you abdicated one of your primary male functions to protect. I wondered how the women in the bloke's family felt about him after this and whether or not he was still allowed the honour of carving the turkey at Christmas . . .

. . . as I was thinking all this, a ball came hurtling towards me and my son. I don't know if it was the reflections I'd just had about public shame, but I was ready to act. I snapped out my forearm in front of my son's head and managed to angle it so that the ball not only *didn't* hit my son but went up, taking the pace off it, and didn't slam into the face of the old bloke behind me.

There was a genuine gasp from around us, not for my reflexes I suspect, but for the idea of what such a pacey shot would've done to a child of his size. So I don't want any credit. No, just doing my job, ma'am.

* Seriously, though, if anyone could source video of that moment I'll pay £1,000 for the footage. Genuine offer, that's why I included the game and date. Contact the publisher.

BLOKEY FILM REVISIONS #4:
STAR WARS

*All of the main male characters from the original
Star Wars trilogy grew up without a father.*

Even as an eight-year-old, I was conscious that the final moments of *Return of the Jedi* had a particular effect on me, but I wouldn't understand why until I became a fully grown man.

As the film reaches its climax, Luke Skywalker – (spoiler alert) son of Darth Vader – is in the throne room of the evil Emperor Palpatine. Luke had believed he could save his father and turn him to the light side of the force, overthrow the emperor and bring peace to the galaxy (a tad optimistic given that the first and only previous meeting with his dad was a few weeks before and Vader chopped off his hand).

Alas, what happens is that his new dad turns Luke over to his boss, then father and son have another big fight. After Luke eventually prevails in the lightsaber duel, the emperor realises the son cannot be turned to the dark side, so tries to finish him off by firing lightning bolts at the young Jedi. Darth Vader, bruised and battered, famously 'more machine now than man', eventually decides he's had enough and lobs the emperor into a giant recycling bin. (This may be a slight oversimplification of the plot.)

When I first saw the film, that particular scene made my whole body come out in goosebumps. Not just the moment of Anakin Skywalker's (Vader's original name) redemption but the swell of

John Williams's incredible score (before George Lucas butchered it by adding in Vader shouting 'Nooooo', like a punter who'd lost money on the favourite at Cheltenham).

There were good reasons why that moment was more resonant for me than my contemporaries. At that time, my relationship with my own father was pretty strained. Not only that, Dad also had a prosthetic limb (though his was from a motorcycle crash rather than a lightsaber duel on a burning pit of lava). Like many dads at the time, my old man was also a bit lost in his work and consequently sometimes sombre around the house. I'm guessing Darth Vader was very much the kind of dad who – if you had friends staying over – would also shout 'don't make me come in there'. However, my dad was way less likely to force-choke someone through a wall.

It took me years to work out why that scene held such power for me. It must have been very odd for my then counsellor when I was talking daddy issues and suddenly blurted out my latest personal revelation – '*I'm* Luke!'

Having written that famous *Return of the Jedi* scene into my own central narrative, I was recently forced to revisit it. With a son of my own and seeing in his eyes the variety of things he needs from me on a daily basis, I started to wonder whether Darth Vader had really earned that redemption after all.

Let's be clear, it takes him quite a long time before he jumps in and saves his son. Luke had already been fairly fried and would probably need ECGs for the rest of his life. And we're not talking about a dilemma between one relative and another – this is between work and your own blood (though admittedly trying to run a galactic empire could count as a passion project). Not only that, but we're just a few short moments down the road from

Vader finding out that Luke has a twin, Princess Leia. His dad's response to learning he has a daughter is to repeat 'Sissssster', like the kind of uncle you wouldn't let babysit. But no, at the very last minute, like an intergalactic version of Jim Carrey in *Liar Liar*, Darth realises he's been going about everything the wrong way and so gets his hero's redemption and is allowed to be one of the cool blue ghosts just before the end credits.

Forget robots and lasers, the theme of fathers and sons is the true engine room of the *Star Wars* saga. Maybe that's the reason why so many blokes of my generation became obsessed with it.

George Lucas's dad was around in his youth but got lost in the day-to-day grind of running a convenience store. They eventually became estranged. So it's probably no coincidence that the three biggest characters in *Star Wars* – Anakin (the artist subsequently known as Darth Vader) Luke and Han Solo – all have daddy issues, though they react to them in very different ways.

It's less prominent in the franchise's extensive mythology, but Han Solo grew up as an orphan, which might be the reason why he has one or two issues with authority. It could also explain why the closest attachment he forms in his life is to a giant rug who makes dog noises.

They're all looking for something to fill that dad-shaped hole. The reason the young Anakin turns to the dark side in the first place is because the evil Chancellor Palpatine is smart enough to realise he's on the look-out for a father figure. He tees up the daddy thing so smartly that I'm surprised the trilogy didn't include a scene where the emperor took him fishing.

Luke is lucky to have a strong father figure around in his uncle

BLOKEY FILM REVISIONS #4: *STAR WARS*

Owen, so is less drawn towards unsavoury types. And when he does put his faith in an older man, its kind old Obi Wan Kenobi, who is more interested in saving planets than blowing them up. Having had decent male role models, when Luke does eventually find out that Darth Vader is his real father (in an epic Jeremy Kyle DNA test in space reveal) he's a bit gutted (I'd imagine it's up there with finding out that your nan's side of the family were Hitlers). And then his hand is lopped off by Vader's lightsaber. Not only is Luke owed years of pocket money, he's also down a few digits.

But by the time the third film starts, Luke has gone all zen about it and just wants to redeem his dear old dad. Maybe he's able to be so evolved due to the positive influence of men like his uncle and Obi Wan (until Obi Wan informs Luke he has to kill his own dad to save the galaxy and is revealed to generally be a bit of a Billy Bullshitter).

I guess, on a subconscious level, my teenage self considered itself very much in the Luke mould. Though I'd had issues with my dad, I could see he'd had a tougher life than me and was doing his best. I understood that losing an arm at such a young age must have been a massive bolt from the blue, in the same way Luke realised that being chopped in half by your best mate might rankle a bit. So I put his emotional distance down to him adding layers of defence after each of the big tragedies which had befallen him. I wanted to get behind my dad's armour to check who was inside.

As part of this mission to rescue him, a couple of years before his death, I resumed hugging him. We'd gone several decades without any kind of tactility beyond a firm handshake and a nod. I'd always presumed that was his preference. However, in another counselling session last year (with my counsellor beginning to wonder if I could discuss any of my feelings without relating them to either *Star Wars* or cricket) my mind released a memory to me, in the same way the CIA sometimes declassify files when they think the public are ready to hear the complicated truths.

I was fourteen and my dad was dropping me back to my mum's house after another one of our stereotypical divorced father-and-son get-togethers at a nearby Burger King. My sister and I had always given Dad a kiss when he dropped us off home, but that night I'd decided something was going to change. We'd had a nice enough time but I told him I wouldn't be kissing him any more, what with me being fourteen and now a big man and all that, so I offered him a handshake instead.

I was too young to understand everything that must have been going on in his mind at that moment. As a dad now, I can speculate on the parental lump in the throat he must have felt on crossing one of those small but devastating thresholds that children pass through. You know they need to evolve, but it can still be crushing as they casually close the door on whole eras.

My emotional spider senses must've logged the atmospherics of the moment, but my hard drive had saved it in the back-up files until I was ready to remember.

I'd always thought my dad stopped hugging me, but it turned out to be the other way around.

I'm not saying we can excuse Darth Vader blowing up whole planets, but sometimes blokes disappear behind their armour because we let them. And for some men, a silly bunch of films about battles in space will do more in unlocking their understanding of themselves than a whole lifetime of counselling.

ME: BINS. YOU: EVERYTHING ELSE FOREVER

The UK public spent £1.7 billion on cards in 2017

Something odd and unspoken happens when a man marries a woman. Yes, there is love, yes, there are the vows you make in the company of friends, family and God, but there's another commitment that never gets said out loud but is usually observed: the woman will take on the responsibility of buying and, probably, sending birthday cards for the bloke's relatives, friends and, in some cases, business associates.

Don't shoot the messenger. I'm not saying this is something the woman formally agrees to or that it's even OK, just that's how it tends to work in most couples. Not just the married or straight ones, either. In any kind of loving partnership, there will be a 'card buyer'. In the heterosexual ones it's almost always the woman.

The phenomenon of birthday calendar responsibility isn't formalised and rarely gets spoken about, it just somehow transpires that, bit by bit, the man will casually outsource this job over time. She will end up at a point where her own iCalendar is dotted with all his important dates, which will look every bit as incongruous as the one for the Battle of the Boyne.

The difference doesn't run along class or cultural lines either. When I rang another comic to speak to her about this idea, she was in the process of writing a card for the sister of her liberal and middle-class husband. It's non-binary, to coin a modern phrase.

And yet it's something which isn't biologically specific to one sex or the other. The ability of women to send birthday cards can't be put on a list alongside breastfeeding.

But why does the birthday card responsibility fall in this manner? Can we claim that holding onto important dates is somehow genetically harder for blokes?

It's a hard line to push, especially when I can tell you the exact date Wimbledon FC beat Liverpool in the FA Cup final. And that I'm more likely to remember Ben Stokes's birthday than my best mate's. We clearly have the power to retain this kind of information but only when it suits us.

Facebook has helped in this respect. Where, once upon a time, birthdays would get missed and the first you'd know of it was when a family member was scowling at you during a christening, Facebook at least affords the chance that, at some point that day, you'll register that several hundred people are making a fuss of someone you love.

But why is it all such hard work for us? Do we simply not care? In fairness, there's a degree of equality to how blokes treat important dates in that we don't make much fuss about our own. The number of people I expect to remember mine is fairly small: my wife, my son, my sister – preferably before 4pm but any time before midnight will do. And that's about it. If my birthday was forgotten my first thought wouldn't be that people didn't care about me, rather that they were busy. Furthermore, as we age, people often excuse the scarcity of the presents bought for blokes by claiming he's 'difficult to buy for'. What that can really mean is that they refuse to buy a man in his mid-forties a virtual reality headset.

The other reason for blokes' crapness in and around cards and gift giving is that we're allowed to get away with it. So perhaps the way to get the message across is for women to perform a bit of tough love. Let him spend a couple of years forgetting the birthdays of everyone close to him, then when his fiftieth birthday is just him standing alone next to some sausage rolls, your point will be made. Perhaps that's a bit extreme but I suspect any change can only come from women saying enough is enough (which I accept is outsourcing change to women to correct the original outsourcing of social responsibilities to women, but that's the way it happened in my house, and I suspect the only way it can happen more broadly, as blokes are inherently lazy if given half a chance).

A few years ago, my wife – given the fact my family is very small and she still has plenty of living relatives to worry about – said that I needed to take over all birthday and social duties for the small number of Norcotts left. I resisted at first and resorted to weak and desperate arguments (at one point stooping so low as to plead that her handwriting simply looked better on birthday cards), but I'm glad she stood her ground.

One of the founding pillars of masculinity is the idea of taking responsibility for your own shit. There's something profoundly babyish about a bloke who wants to hand all that stuff over to his Mrs . . . for *life*.

I'll admit, it's been a long road, with one or two bumps along the way. And yes, some cards have needed to be couriered because I've remembered so late. It's also true that possibly as many as 60 per cent of cards are opened with the price tag still on. And I have made liberal use of online card sellers, like Moonpig.

(Moonpig, by the way, is a great option for blokes but you need to be careful when using the card designs as they often have default settings. I still owe my sister an apology for when I left a proforma entry on and she received a birthday card for the mysterious 'Stephanie'. Though I was afforded far more latitude than any of my female family members would've received for making the same mistake.)

It doesn't just stop at birthday cards either: women will also keep a general overview of what's going on in the lives of the people around them. They'll remember the names of any new babies (I'm OK with the first two but if any couple are selfish enough to have a third I often refer to it as 'third baby').

While I've made great strides in card sending, I've still got a long way to go in terms of being across the information side of things. In a typical moment familiar to many married couples, we'll often park up to visit family or friends and the last ten steps from the car to the front door will resemble a weird presidential briefing, with my wife as the clued-up advisor trying to make sure her very own version of Joe Biden doesn't put his foot in it. She'll have a lot of information to relay in a short space of time, much of which will be things not to say, but as they are often things I wasn't aware of in the first place, an argument will ensue regarding whether it was foolish to let me in on such 'state secrets'. I'm pretty sure no American president has ever been in possession of the actual state secrets – you can't trust one bloke with something that important. In the same way, I can't be trusted with gossip about someone being a 'weekend lesbian'.

The social stuff might be harder to crack, but for everything else, the good news for blokes is that technology has made life significantly easier. Not just in terms of purchasing cards online or repeat reminders on the iCalendar, but the actual process of buying presents. You can nip on a website like Amazon and type in some fairly easy searches. All you need to remember is the sex of the person you're buying for and their age (OK, the second one might be tricky for some blokes, but shoot ballpark and you won't go far wrong).

You can even type in 'presents for middle-aged women'. My big tip here is never to go for the suggestions on the first page. Women are smart so you could at least put in some effort. I'd recommend starting with at least page four. The last thing you'd want them to think is that you're a bit lazy.

HEROES OF BLOKEDOM #5: MY MATE MICK

The last of my blokey heroes is another person I've had the pleasure of knowing, but he's an everyday hero rather than one in the public eye.

I first met Mick in the mid-eighties when my mum divorced my dad but decided to leave him with the house and move us to a council estate in Wimbledon (an interesting strategy which must have confused her solicitor). Most people wouldn't associate Wimbledon with the idea of council estates, but it's not all strawberries and small houses which cost more than a condo in Beverley Hills – back then it had its dodgy areas too. (If this gritty milieu is of interest to you, I heartily recommend my memoir, *Where Did I Go Right?*, available in all good bookshops.)

On the estate, I suffered the incongruity of everyone I met elsewhere thinking where I lived was 'posh', despite having both a football club and a greyhound stadium on my doorstep. These are two nailed-on horsemen of the 'shit area' apocalypse; the third is that you're living above a nail salon or a bookies.

There were some boisterous kids on this estate, so I quickly palled up with a much calmer proposition: Michael Edmonds. Mick. His character beamed out and – even as a kid – I recognised him as possessing the qualities you find in what most people would consider to be an excellent bloke.

Mick liked music, football and fast food. He liked a laugh and didn't take himself too seriously, plus he enjoyed occasionally going out on the smash. We were always going to get along. The eldest of six, he was a caring older brother who pitched in with raising his siblings. They loved and depended on him at a deeper level than just that of a brother. In the same way, I came to rely on him as so much more than just a friend.

Mick was calm, helpful, patient and, like all proper blokes, could actually build and fix stuff. One day, I got hammered and locked myself out of the flat we were living in. In my drunken state, I thought I could barge through the back door and get away with only damaging the small metal lock, which would be easy enough to fix once I'd sobered up. In the event, I took the whole door off, half the frame and a good chunk of the wall and plaster. Mick came back from a long day at work (actual manual work), surveyed the damage and got straight down to the repairs. He never once bollocked me or even took the piss.

The very least I deserved was a new door-based nickname.

Sadly, it is often the case that nice guys don't get the breaks they deserve. Mick died shortly before his fortieth birthday, survived by two fantastic sons and a loving wife.

A nice bloke, a calm bloke, dependable, handy and loyal – if you were ever looking for the definitive good bloke, look no further than my mate Mick.

HOLIDAYS

I have, in my line of work, done a lot of travelling, meaning I've spent a fair bit of time in airports. Sitting alone, you do more people-watching than usual. One of my guilty pleasures is clocking just how many blokes seem to be getting told off by their partners in departure lounges. It's the most basic kind of schadenfreude: I know what it feels like to be that guy and I'm glad that today it's not me.

Couples flying without kids row too, but the stresses of having children around makes a showdown outside W H Smith far more likely. And, as you'd expect, those tiffs are more pronounced when taking early flights. You can see it's been a bastard of a morning for all involved and we can reasonably presume the woman has done more to make the holiday happen. Yes, the dad might have done what he thinks of as the 'project management' end of the planning: heroically worked out how many Avios they had in the household account when booking the break and – without a thought for his own personal safety – checked the travel insurance covered Turks and Caicos, but even on the actual day of the holiday, the woman is likely to have been the busier of the two – wrangling children and supplies while the bloke stares at the 'live departures board' on his phone like that's an actual job. When you see a grown man getting a dressing-down from his wife outside

Boots, it's likely to be the culmination of a week where he didn't help packing then spent the morning of departure wandering around like a tit in a trance, hoping that the complex endeavour of getting a dog to kennels and three small children to another country would somehow magically occur.

I can't help but find the spectacle a bit funny. There's the bloke, his pleading arms outstretched, a dumb look on his face, like a man who ignored warnings of a gale now realising that it's a hurricane.

I saw one of these dressing-downs recently at Heathrow Terminal 5. The woman tore an absolute strip off her bloke, proper Sir Alex Ferguson stuff. I thought she might even sub him at halftime. This would have been a very different moment if the guy had been verbally laying into his Mrs. If he'd have raised his voice that loud for long enough, someone might have intervened. But the bloke took it. Why?

Firstly, he was smart enough to know that the well-being of his family unit in transit will be enhanced if he takes his medicine and lets her get it out of her system. He could pull the nuclear option and say, 'Fuck this, don't speak to me like that, I'm going to the Wetherspoons for a pint.' But sadly, it's not the seventies any more.

Sorry, I mean, happily, it's not the seventies any more.

The fact that the woman probably did the majority of packing won't have helped. I don't know many blokes – even among my most feminist mates – who pack for their own holiday. Equality is one thing but their other halves aren't yet at the point where they'll trust him to know the right clothes for ten days in Cape Verde. However, what seems like incompetence can just come down to different priorities. Left to his own devices, a bloke will often think of the stress of getting shitloads of heavy luggage from the house to the airport and beyond. Consequently, he may decide that two pairs of shorts for an entire holiday will suffice, imagining that he'll rinse and dry them in the hotel room, like a Poundland Ant Middleton.

The other reason blokes may not be asked to do something as important as packing is that they were allowed to once and made an absolute hash of it – which brings into play the murky area of 'constructive incompetence'. Constructive incompetence isn't so much doing things deliberately badly, it's more allowing our natural lack of common sense to do the work for us. I genuinely wonder whether Kwasi Kwarteng wasn't doing this during his time as chancellor. To me – a bloke well-versed in constructive incompetence – that definitely looked like the actions of a man who never wanted to run the economy again.

As with so many aspects of blokery, our crapness in some areas means we need to make up for them in the areas in which we are still relied upon. The 'pre-holiday admin' should be the bloke's domain. Not just the aforementioned booking of hotels, but the relevant visas, ESTAs and inoculations. (I realise most of these are things you can do on your phone while sitting on the couch with terrible posture, but it's a start.)

The holiday admin workload went up exponentially for anyone who dared to fly during the pandemic. I almost cocked this up and my wife and I ended up having to test twice in twenty-four hours, which made us look either paranoid or incompetent.

Then there's picking a restaurant in a foreign country, a process which sometimes means you have to compromise between your desire to have exactly what you want and the pragmatic demands of feeding a small person. You may want the place with the good reviews, but sometimes the child is screaming for the kind of calories which haven't appeared on any TripAdvisor top tens. In a situation like this, never be the guy who says, as I once did: 'But babe, that place is only a 3.5. Do you know how many twos a place would need to average 3.5? If we just walk another mile there's a cracking 4.2.'

My big tip for holidays is to arrange a surprise airport transfer. These days, it can be as cheap as booking an Uber when you get there. Whatever uselessness you may have exhibited in the build-up to departure, you can pull it all back if, after a long and stressful flight, you come out of arrivals to a bloke holding up an iPad with your name on it. A lot may be forgiven. And if you've just remembered you left your child's beloved iPad on the plane, all that can wait until you get to the hotel bar.

THE DEATH OF DIY

Eighty-nine per cent of over fifty-fives can change a lightbulb compared to just sixty-three per cent of eighteen- to twenty-four-year-olds.

Historians often chart the big changes in society via high-profile tectonic geopolitical shifts. The abdication of a monarch, wars, a new prime minister (though the gloss has recently come off this particular phenomenon). For ordinary people, however, while those kinds of changes do register, the things which really stick in the collective memory and actually change life at ground level can be more everyday – like pound notes going out of circulation, mandatory seat belts, and the rapid disappearance of cash as a legitimate form of payment.

I experienced that kind of small but seismic moment recently when a friend who works in the car industry told me that most new standard model cars no longer come with a spare wheel. I asked him why and he explained that there are a number of reasons, like cost and space, but high among them is the reality that people whose tyres do have a puncture are now very unlikely to set about the task of resolving the issue themselves.

I asked him if by 'people' he meant 'blokes'. He repeated the word 'people' defensively because he's one of those successful modern boardroom types who has risen to great prominence by not always acknowledging the part that statistical likelihood plays in the real world.

I took this dismal DIY news badly. I understood the disappearance of spare wheels from the boots of cars as an assault on all blokery. Basically, the car industry had taken one look at us and gone: 'Nah. Not for you boys, eh? Why don't you go sit on the grass verge and wait for a real man to come and sort it out. Maybe journal how this whole experience made you feel.'

I was concerned, but I am also a part of the reason a decision like that had been made. Because, while luckily I've never experienced a flat tyre while driving, if I am honest with myself, can I genuinely say I'd have gone through the process of setting my hazard sign fifty yards down the hard shoulder and got to work by the side of a busy road? Would I have known how to use the . . . I was going to write about the tools I'd have used but I don't even know what they're called.

It's shameful, really. My old man wasn't the handiest bloke in the world but if he couldn't have done something as simple as change a tyre, he'd have handed back his man card immediately. And he only had one arm.

Even if I somehow managed to fit a spare wheel, there would be a cold, silent drive home as neither my wife nor son would have any faith that I'd executed the task safely.

So alas, I have to admit, if I'd experienced a flat tyre at any time in the twenty-six years I've been driving I would have been on the phone to the AA just like the rest of them (except I'd have adopted a Terry Jones-style lady's voice to hide my shame and get a quicker call-out).

So what has gone on in the last few decades? Is the phenomenon of blokes becoming crap at DIY an unequivocal stain on my generation? Is there a general change of tide when it comes to building or fixing things?

Someone performing car surgery by the side of a busy road might in fact seem like something of an anachronism in this increasingly risk-averse age. In a world in which people have spent a couple of years wearing masks on public transport, can we handle the shock of seeing a bloke in a business suit under a Renault Picasso by the A40? It might register like one of those blithe two fingers to health and safety from a bygone age, such as seeing a pregnant woman smoking. While she changes a tyre.

The dissipation of DIY skills isn't without context. The last decade has also seen a rise in the number of people using dedicated builders of flat-pack furniture. Yes, flat-pack assembly, the angry epitome of blokeiness, is routinely being outsourced to men who come to your house and assemble furniture for you.

Where does it stop? Do we get stronger men in to carve the Christmas turkey? Will we start hiring professional barbecuers? (As I write this, I'm picturing women, tired of cremated chicken and food poisoning, weighing up the pros and cons.)

Before I seem too fusty and conservative, there's a practical reason why men should lament how this generation of blokes has drifted away from DIY. One area in which we definitely have the edge on women is physical strength. And when women are living more independent lives and enjoying ever greater earning power, men simply have to deliver in the few fields where we still hold a natural advantage.

This isn't to say that there aren't strong women who can put their own furniture together – more that, in terms of the statistical average, we have a little bit more torque strength when it comes to screwing and tightening bolts. Blokes, we have to own this USP because if we don't the market will decide.

There's an actual website called 'Hire a Hubby'. Currently, they limit themselves to household maintenance, but how long before women start making requests on other occasions when a bloke could come in useful? Like renting a man to be the plus-one at a wedding. Or getting a day lease on a fella for that bit at airports between getting the luggage out of the car and checking in.

On the whole, marriage provides significantly more benefits for men in terms of general well-being. Having a bloke can arguably be socially convenient for a woman, but there being someone around to kill spiders won't help her to live longer.

This is the cold, hard transactional reality of the male–female marriage dynamic. So it's imperative that if a tyre needs to be changed or a radiator has to be bled, in this small handful of circumstances, blokes provide a reminder that our presence still makes life a bit easier.

Simply put, if a bloke doesn't make himself useful on occasion, then his very existence is under threat.

Don't worry , the DIY doesn't have to be the high-level stuff. You're unlikely to be asked to build something as complex as a cupboard. It could just be the odd nod in the general direction of that duty.

Recently, and without prompting, I noticed that the door handle barrel (I had to google the name for it) was starting to come a bit loose. And so . . . I fixed it! Did I use a breadknife instead of finding the correct screwdriver? Perhaps, but the point is that I dealt with it.

I was on a roll then and so pulled out the WD-40 to manfully address a squeaky upstairs door. What happened next was magical – my wife brought me sandwiches like I was a returning Viking conqueror. I've now gone from avoiding DIY to actively looking for things to fix.

LET IT ALL OUT

*Crying only once every few months was reported by
27 per cent of men, while 47 per cent of women said
they cry once a month.*

The capacity and willingness to cry changes a lot over the course
of a bloke's life. When we're little boys we cry easily as much as
girls, arguably more. Boys' peculiar tendency towards solipsism
means there's the feeling that – along with all the standard things
children blub over, like grazed knees or having to wash any part
of their body, ever – every lost board game or inability to
immediately master some new and complex skill is just cause to
turn on the waterworks.

Little boys cry a lot but there comes a point when those boys
start becoming men and these feelings are managed downwards
to avoid looking weak.

I can hear the liberals trilling, 'But crying isn't weak, it's
actually a sign of strength!' It can be, but as a bloke, you've got
to be realistic about the frequency with which it can happen.

Women have more liberty when it comes to crying in public.
During my time working in offices, the occasional crying woman
was a common staple of working life. It would often happen on
a Wednesday afternoon, for some reason. The day would be
drifting aimlessly towards 5pm when you'd suddenly hear
sniffling in the corner. The other women in the office – blessed
with an ability to animatedly mouth things wordlessly across a

room – would try to get the attention of the hitherto heedless blokes sitting closest to poor old Janine.

'Ja-nine is cry-ing in the cor-ner,' they'd carefully mouth.

The blokes, not recognising the attendant quiet protocols, would shout back, 'WHAT'S WRONG WITH JANINE?'

Some of the most emotionally retentive fellas sitting nearest to the stricken Janine would start to look agitated, turning around, trying to call in female air-support. 'Could some of the women DO something about this please?' their pleading eyes would say. 'I've asked her if she's alright, she said she was fine. I don't see what more *I can do at this juncture.*'

Female colleagues would duly support their fallen sister in the form of a team of first responders on the scene, who'd spirit Janine away for some chat and understanding while the blokes would breathe a huge sigh of relief.

One woman would always mysteriously return for her bag. I never found out what that bag contained, but always presumed it was tampons or Valium.

I probably sit in the middle ground in terms of my blokey capacity for empathy. In the workplace, I'd generally rather people kept their emotions in check, but if they do have an issue I won't pretend nothing's happening. Not all blokes are like this.

In the mid-nineties, I was working in an office with one other lad. Our line manager was an Antipodean girl called Kirsty, a nice girl and very mild-mannered.

One Wednesday afternoon (of course), Kirsty came into our small office and straight away I could tell she was ticking. My fundamental selfishness made me consider glossing over it, but I eventually checked, 'Are you OK?'

This question can be a catalyst when you're not OK, the glint of human empathy can tip you over the edge, and sure enough, it all came flooding out. She'd had a brutal board meeting where they'd torn a strip off her and she needed to have a bit of a cry.

I sat down next to her to talk about what had happened and do the sensible thing of agreeing that yes, they were all arseholes and *of course* she was awesome and they didn't know how *lucky* they were to have her (even if I broadly concurred with some of their criticisms of Kirsty's frankly flaky management style).

My colleague, Grant, asked if she wanted a cup of tea. Kirsty thanked him but said no. He asked again a couple of minutes later and she said no again. He asked a third time and I realised the tea wasn't really for Kirsty, Grant just wanted to get out of there, so I said, 'Actually, I'll have one mate . . . and can you get it from the café . . . by the Prince of Wales?'

For his own good, I sent him as far as I reasonably could to get that tea. He may still be waiting around the corner to see if the coast is clear.

Male emotions in public have a premium based on their scarcity, which is why when a male sports star cries after a major sporting event it can hold a lot of power. We understand that he's worked so hard for this moment that, with the task at hand successfully concluded, he has finally allowed the dam to break. Those tears aren't rolling down his cheek, they're *escaping* against his better judgement. This is allowable male crying – he's earned it.

That might sound harsh but imagine Rafa Nadal being interviewed after getting through the second round of

Wimbledon against a lowly ranked wildcard and suddenly bursting into tears. You'd be thinking, 'OK, bit weird, Rafa, but maybe you've had a tricky day.' If he proceeded to do that after every round, and sometimes during training, you'd start questioning whether Rafa needed some time away from hitting balls.

If you're a blokey bloke, go ahead and have the odd cry, but be aware that it's an act that – if you don't do it very often – you're not going to look especially comfortable doing. Just like our old coot near the beginning of the book cack-handedly applying suntan lotion to the awkward bit of his lower back, men who rarely cry finally having a blub can look, well, *ugly*. Because they don't do it often, when the tears do finally come it's a whole body experience. Rather than bleeding the radiators, they've opened the door on a walk-in bath filled to the brim.

When my wife has a little cry she can – somewhat incredibly – still multitask. She'll also be talking, wiping away tears and, on some occasions, continuing to fold clothes. When I was going through a sad period, however, my crying was visceral and primitive, like I wasn't just having a little blub but was engaged in the painful process of becoming the Hulk. My body contorted and convulsed; I looked to be in physical pain. It must have been an awful sight, so fair play to her for continuing to listen and not turning the hose on me.

Since my mum passed, I've become a late convert to crying. What the repressed me hadn't realised was that it isn't just for when you feel sad, it can be for other emotions too, like anxiety or frustration. So I love a good cry now. It's cathartic. Lads, we cannot let women walk around holding this strategic advantage.

The feeling after a good cry is incredible. I feel calmer, happier – the world even looks more colourful.

In fact, I've got so attached to that refreshing feeling that if I'm off out on a big day or setting off for an important work event, I'll often ask myself if I could crank out a quick cry beforehand – a bit like the emotional equivalent of a tactical chunder during a day on the piss.

So when we talk about blokes crying, let's not descend into platitudes and pretend that it's exactly the same rules as for women. I'm a firm believer in the restorative power of a good cry, but also think it's OK if the majority of that is done in private. You can have too much of a good thing.

My big fear for blokery throughout this book has been that, in trying to adapt and fit in with a fast-changing modern world, we lose some of the useful stuff. And the complicated truth about blokes crying in public is that it's good to do it sometimes, but take a hint from the tennis players and save it for the big games rather than the qualifying rounds.

'I've always said that if my son thinks of me as one of his idiot friends, I'll have succeeded as a dad.'

Phil Dunphy,
Modern Family

EPILOGUE

When I was writing the last chapter of this book, it occurred to me that, despite my own qualified support for blokes' right to have a good cry, my son might have reached the age of six and a half without having seen me shed a single tear.

So I asked him. 'Son, have you ever seen me cry?'

He looked up from his Lego. 'No. No, I don't think I have.' (This might seem wordy, but his sentences are often structured like those of the nice guy in a Jane Austen novel.)

'I do sometimes,' I said, 'I do cry . . . you know that, right?'

He nodded and seemed to be in an open mood, so I pushed the subject a little further. 'What do you think you'd do if you did see me cry?'

Very quickly he said, 'I'd tell you to get out!' and pointed to the door.

He must've registered the shock on my face because he immediately came over and sought to reassure me that it was just a joke.

Not only that, the phrase 'get out!' is one I often use when pretending to be angry with him for a comically minor transgression. He was just echoing it back to me for a laugh.

Like all novice pranksters, he was a bit alarmed that his joke had worked too well, and reassured me, 'Daddy, if you were really crying I would just ask you what was wrong.'

Beautiful, right?

A good kid, but also one who now clearly understood the principles of banter.

And not only that, but when to stop.

I don't know what the future is for blokes generally, but if they're anything like my brilliant son, that future will be in very safe hands.

SOURCES

Display quotations

Homer J Simpson, from the TV show *The Simpsons*, Season 5, Episode 18, 'Burns' Heir' (1994)

Forrest Gump, from the film *Forrest Gump* (The Tisch Company/Paramount Pictures, dir. Robert Zemeckis, 1994)

Mrs Doubtfire, from the film *Mrs. Doubtfire* (20th Century Fox/Blue Wolf Productions, dir. Chris Columbus, 1993)

Daddy Pig, from the TV show *Peppa Pig*, Season 4, Episode 3, 'Basketball' (2011)

Don Corleone, from the film *The Godfather* (Paramount Pictures/Alfran Productions, dir. Francis Ford Coppola, 1972)

Apollo Creed, from the film *Rocky III* (United Artists/Chartoff-Winkler Productions, dir. Sylvester Stallone, 1982)

Phil Dunphy, from the TV show *Modern Family*, Season 3, Episode 4, 'Door to Door' (2011)

Chapter openers

British men do approximately half the amount of housework of their female counterparts. 'It's official! Study shows women do 70 minutes more housework each day than men', by Victoria Allen, *MailOnline*, 10 March 2022. https://www.dailymail.co.uk/news/article-10596575/British-women-doing-70-minutes-household-chores-day-men.html

On holiday, 82 per cent of women wear sun cream, versus only 65 per cent of men . . . who are probably acting under strict instruction. 'Sunscreen/sun tan lotion usage in Great Britain 2017, by gender', published by Dominique Petruzzi, 2 February 2022. https://www.statista.com/statistics/750001/sun-tan-lotion-usage-by-gender-in-great-britain-uk/

More than half of British men gamble. 'New research shows almost half of people in Britain gamble', Gambling Commission, 28 February 2017. https://www.gamblingcommission.gov.uk/news/article/new-research-shows-almost-half-of-people-in-britain-gamble

Supporting the football team your dad followed is the top reason people pick a side. 'Reasons why football fans choose who to support – from team's kit to family', by Sarah Lumley, Mirror.co.uk, 12 May 2022. https://www.mirror.co.uk/sport/football/reasons-football-fans-choose-who-26942614

The average age at which British men lose their virginity is 18.3 years old. 'At what age did Britons lose their virginity?', by Peter Raven, 1 March 2023. https://yougov.co.uk/topics/society/articles-reports/2023/03/01/what-age-did-britons-lose-their-virginity#:~:text=Men%20are%20slightly%20more%20likely,compared%20to%202017%20for%20women

Five foot nine is the average height for a UK male. 'Average Height by Country 2023', World Population Review. https://worldpopulationreview.com/country-rankings/average-height-by-country

What do you think you'd have been if you weren't a footballer? legendary Peter Crouch interview that has been acknowledged by him in numerous subsequent interviews.

Women make 50 per cent more visits to the doctors per year than men. 'Are men less likely to visit their GP than women?', by Dr Jen Tan, A. Vogel, 17 October 2018. https://www.avogel.co.uk/health/mens-health/are-men-less-likely-to-visit-their-gp-than-women/#:~:text=On%20average%2C%20men%20visit%20their,suffering%20from%20a%20serious%20problem

Man flu definition. 'Man Flu', Wikipedia, accessed 20 June 2023. https://en.wikipedia.org/wiki/Man_flu

The average age at which British men become a father is 33.7. 'Birth characteristics in England and Wales: 2021', Office for National Statistics, 19 January 2023. https://www.ons.gov.uk/peoplepopulationandcommunity/birthsdeathsandmarriages/livebirths/bulletins/birthcharacteristicsinenglandandwales/2021

Eight per cent of UK men only cook from scratch once a month. 'How often do you cook from scratch?', published by Nils-Gerrit Wunsch, Statistica.com, 30 November 2021. https://www.statista.com/statistics/1140395/frequency-of-cooking-from-scratch-by-gender-uk/

Forty-one per cent of British men say they have friends they 'like but don't bother to see' 'YouGov Big Friendship Survey', YouGov.co.uk, 16 December 2021. https://docs.cdn.yougov.com/byav0wzw4d/You-

Gov%20-%20The%20Big%20Friendship%20Survey.pdf

Women file for 62 per cent of all divorces in England and Wales. 'Divorces in England and Wales: 2021', Office for National Statistics, 2 November 2022. https://www.ons.gov.uk/peoplepopulationand-community/birthsdeathsandmarriages/divorce/bulletins/divorcesinen glandandwales/2021#:~:text=Among%20opposite%2Dsex%20cou-ples%20in,and%2037.4%25%20with%20males%20petitioning

The average erect penis in the UK is 5.17 inches. 'The average penis size for a male isn't as big as you think', by Annie Hayes, *Men's Health*, 5 December 2022. https://www.menshealth.com/uk/sex/a25932392/average-penis-size-uk/

Women can have visible abs with 14 to 20 per cent body fat, while men's needs to be as low as 6 to 13 per cent. 'How long does it take to get abs? And how to speed up the process', by Emmie Satrazemis, *Trifecta*, 26 June 2021. https://www.trifectanutrition.com/blog/how-long-does-it-take-to-get-abs

The average British man gets married at thirty-two. 'All you need is love (and a marriage certificate): Marriage since 1900', *Olympic Britain: Social and economic change since the 1908 and 1948 London Games*, 10 July 2012. https://www.parliament.uk/cont entassets/004e41737ee74530af256372e5e6840b/olympicbritain. pdf#page=37

Ten per cent of British men think they could beat a chimpanzee in a fight with their bare hands. 'Which animals could Britons beat in a fight?', by Matthew Smith, yougov.co.uk, 21 May 2021. https://you-gov.co.uk/topics/society/articles-reports/2021/05/21/which-animals-could-britons-beat-fight

All of the main male characters from the original Star Wars trilogy grew up without a father.

The UK public spent £1.7 billion on cards in 2017. Greeting Card Association's 2018 market report. www.gca.cards

Eighty-nine per cent of over fifty-fives can change a lightbulb compared to just 63 per cent of eighteen to twenty-four-year-olds. 'The decline of the UK's DIY skills', *Insight DIY*, 3 October 2018. https://www.insightdiy.co.uk/news/the-decline-of-the-uks-diy-skills/6533.htm

Crying only once every few months was reported by 27 per cent of men, while 47 per cent of women said they cry once a month. 'Cry like a man: How women really want their men to show emotion', by Dani-Elle Dubé, Global News, 22 February 2018. https://globalnews. ca/news/4039294/cry-like-a-man-how-women-really-want-their-men-to-show-emotion/

ABOUT THE AUTHOR

Writer and comedian Geoff Norcott is well known for his TV work on *Question Time, Live At The Apollo, Backstage With Katherine Ryan, Late Night Mash, Mock The Week* and *Have I Got News For You.* He has also fronted his own documentary, *How The Middle Class Ruined Britain,* for BBC2.

A regular on Radio 4, he's known for his comedy specials and won the 2019 BBC Radio & Music Award. Geoff often appears on Times Radio and is also the host of the popular podcast *What Most People Think.*

His first book *Where Did I Go Right? How The Left Lost Me* was published in May 2021 by Monoray.